Also by *ANDY RUSSELL:*

Grizzly Country
Trails of a Wilderness Wanderer
Adventures with Wild Animals

HORNS
in the High Country

HORNS
in the
High Country

ANDY RUSSELL

Douglas & McIntyre
Vancouver/Toronto

Printed in the United States of America

10 9 8 7 6 5 4 3 2 1

Douglas & McIntyre Ltd., 1615 Venables Street,
Vancouver, British Columbia V5L 2H1

Published in arrangement with Alfred A. Knopf, Inc.
Published simultaneously in the United States by
Nick Lyons Books.

Canadian Cataloguing in Publication Data

Russell, Andy, 1915–
Horns in the high country.

Originally published: New York: Knopf, 1973.
ISBN 0-88894-549-3

1. Mountain sheep.   2. Rocky Mountain goat.
I. Title.
QL737.U53R88   1987   599.73′58   C87-091054-X

Dedicated to the memory of

BERT RIGGALL,

and those many friends who

shared our fires

Contents

Introduction

There is nothing quite so satisfying to the soul as walking or riding through wild sheep and mountain goat country, especially in the fall after the first frost. The air is tangy with the smell of ripe growth and timberline trees, and on a clear day you can see a hundred miles or more from the top of a high ridge. It is rugged country, with cloud shadows chasing one another over the mountains. It is exhilarating to breath and feel one's blood flowing while watching these master climbers as they go about their lives.

But how traumatic it is to go back to a well-remembered place after a long absence, expecting to renew a vision of mountain wonderland, to find it scarred with logging roads and vast piles of wrecked trees dotted with stumps of a clear-cut. Perhaps a few bighorns still use the high meadows, but the goats are long gone, for they will not tolerate the noise. It is as though a curtain has been lowered—a curtain painted with destruction. The idea that cutting timber in such a fashion improves the range for the grazers and browsers is a myth.

Hunting overharvest is bad, but the degradation of suitable habitat for wildlife is much worse, for up here it takes hundreds of years to grow a fair sized tree.

There are many youngsters being born now in the shadows of the mountains who will never know the sight of wild sheep and mountain goats playing and feeding on the slopes as we did only a few short years ago. The ice-carved contours of the ridges and valleys are the same, but in too many places the thin skin of top soil is gone, a layer of soil, many thousands of years in the making. Up here where the air is thin and dry, it can be a decade before a pine needle turns into soil and if there isn't a pine to supply it, the process stretches into countless generations. For now, when the winter snowpack melts in spring, it goes with a rush instead of trickling down all summer to feed the rivers. With the flood goes the old grass, leaves and rotten wood that would make new soil. We build dams to control the floods we cause and the lakes above the dams fill up with silt. It is a progression of error and the reason for deserts. It is not just sheep and goats that suffer, but every other living thing as well, including us, for we are fast putting ourselves on the danger list being compiled by our plundering and greed.

I have pitched my tent in wild country untouched by anything heavier than boots or hooves from Idaho north to Alberta and British Columbia, through parts of the Northwest Territories and the Yukon into the central mountains of Alaska. I have shared many campfires with friends through storm and sunshine, where the clouds play around mountain peaks standing like teeth against the sky. Once it was easy to dodge the competition of wheels, but not any more.

A couple of university students and I undertook to do so in 1974, when we walked through the country between Jasper Park, Alberta, and Waterton Lakes Park on the international border four hundred miles to the south. We were carrying fifty pound packs and largely living on freeze-dried food, which sustained us but is not my idea of living very high when it comes to groceries. We deliberately picked routes too rough for even horses, for that is about the only way to keep away from traffic and the sound of heavy industry outside the national parks. It was hard work but worth it, and at the end of that journey we were about as fit and tough as any three people can ever get.

To be sure, the goats and sheep are still there, though we did not see them in anything like the numbers they were throughout the mountains twenty years before. It was cheering, late one afternoon following a long day of climbing, to spot three big old rams. They were high on a craggy shoulder behind Tornado Mountain, up on the headwaters of an unnamed creek just over the continental divide from the top of the Oldman River watershed. All wore full-curl, massive horns, but the leader of that bachelor's club was the biggest and heaviest I have ever seen in sixty years of wandering the mountains. They were bedded down in some high shelves, their beds carefully chosen to command every point of the compass. Nothing could have moved within half a mile of them without being seen. They had not grown so old and big by taking chances.

That great herdmaster was never killed by a hunter or it would have made headlines and the world's record broken. Somewhere up in that wild craggy country, where the winds play and roar, there is a bleached-out skull and horns marking the last resting place of a great ram—maybe the mightiest of them all.

Who knows? Some day when the last call comes and I too trail up over the pass to spirit land, I may meet him again. If I do, I will know him there among the wild and the free, where the smoke of the campfire lifts against a backdrop of mountains and the crystal clear waters of natural fountains leap and play among mountain flowers.

—Andy Russell
Turner Valley, Alberta
December, 1986

Foreword

It has occurred to me that it might be better to have someone else not so close to this story write an introduction; but in viewing the highly personal nature of the account, the telling of a big portion of my life spent observing, hunting and living with the horned wild ones of the Rockies, perhaps it is more fitting for me to launch it. Certainly nobody knows better than I the great depth of feeling experienced while following many thousands of miles of trails through mountain wilderness reaching across the Canadian west and north into interior Alaska. It is thus I have made my living by one means or another all closely associated with the life of the wild creatures. It is here I went to school, and here where I came to realize that men are not so superior they can afford to overlook their links with other kinds of life, or the powerful pattern that holds it all together.

For the inveterate storyteller, writing such a book is more than just sitting down to one's typewriter with some material and an idea, it is a compulsion growing inside a man until it becomes impossible to contain it any more. And while this account may at times seem like the nostalgic recall of one who mourns the wonderful old days when the wilderness stretched unbroken for thousands of miles from his door, the primitive joy of being a part of it, the vastness, and the pristine beauty, it is also a plea to the reader to stand up and be counted in helping preserve something of what is left. It fulfills a desire to illustrate the features of a beautifully rugged land termed as wild sheep country and shared by many other associated species, in the hope that my interpretation of things seen will help readers appreciate the many irreplaceable features which we can still lose by failing to care about them. Much of the country described in this book has been destroyed since I first rambled the wild ram pastures and climbed the narrow ledges behind the whiskery mountain goats, and no change of heart can restore it. Only nature can build wilderness country. Man can easily take it apart, but he cannot rebuild it.

Many of the people mentioned herein are dead and those who are left that remember the wild trails no longer have much elasticity left in their legs, but their memories are good.

No man writing such a book does so alone and I wish to thank those who have so generously assisted me, although their contributions are largely indirect. Sources of information have been wide and varied and are listed as follows: *The Bighorn Sheep in the United States, Its Past, Present and Future* by Helmut K. Buechner; *The Great Arc of the Wild Sheep* by James L. Clark; *Hunting in the Upper Yukon* and *The Wilderness of the Denali* by Charles Sheldon; *Mountain Sheep* by Valerius

Geist. My thanks also to some good friends of the trail, Jack O'Connor and Warren Page, whose various books and accounts in *Outdoor Life* and *Field and Stream* have added to the store of knowledge, as well as Colonel Harry Snyder, author of *Big Game Hunting*.

Some of the material used in this book has been previously published in article form in *Outdoor Life*, *Field and Stream*, *True*, *Reader's Digest* and *The American Sportsman*. I owe a debt of gratitude to these various publications for their encouragement and support to the efforts of this wilderness scribe over a period of twenty-seven years.

It would be an unforgivable oversight not to mention Ernest Thomson Seton, whose various works—including *Krag, The Kootenai Ram*, which was set in the mountains here just back of our ranch—originally put flame in the firebox of my desire both to become a naturalist and to write about wildlife.

If writing has done anything for me, it has won me some great friends. Paramount among these is Angus Cameron, whose gentle reining has done much to help me avoid the literary badger holes one is apt to put his foot in and fall on his face. As my editor he has offered valuable advice, not all of which has been accepted without argument, but nonetheless greatly appreciated. There have likely been times when he was sure he was dealing with a tough, ornery and uncompromising savage, but through it all a friendship has developed, forged and welded in the atmosphere of our mutual interest in creative work.

HORNS
in the High Country

1

The Land of
the Sky

The basin is like a great bowl with one side broken out in a jagged gap towards the east, where the creek draining the place takes a dizzy plunge fifteen hundred feet into the canyon below, and then goes twisting down between the mountains towards the Waterton River. For want of a better name we will call it Paradise Basin, which is whispering-close to adequate, because surely this place is a mountain heaven open to the early morning sun, and walled off on its remaining three sides by peaks, cliffs and snow-strewn talus fans. With its five lakes tied together by clear cold creeks and roaring white-water cascades, its vast hanging gardens with little fountains playing among hundreds of kinds of alpine flowers—all forming magnificent timberline pastures for bighorns, mountain goats, mule deer and the grizzly bear that sometimes lives there in summer—it is a kind of magnificently serene Rocky Mountain paradise.

This day was blazing hot—much hotter than usual in early August, the sun pouring down and glinting off the facets of little waves stirring the surface of the lake in front of me. Sitting with my back comfortably propped against a small alpine fir tree in the cool shade of a bigger one, I idly watched a solitary sandpiper as it pirouetted and curtsied in pursuit of some tiny insects hatching among the water-washed pebbles of the beach a few feet ahead of my outstretched boots.

My fly rod leaned forgotten against the tree beside me. I had been out since early morning—just in time to see the beginning of a tremendous hatch of small black gnats that had brought the trout to the surface in a frenzy of feeding. The insects were so tiny my fly box was hard pressed to match them, but a minute version of a parachute fly simply tied, with no other dressing than three or four wraps of a single black hackle on a number sixteen long shank hook, proved adequate. It floated exactly like a miniature umbrella with the crook of its handle hanging below the surface, and while it in no way appeared to match the insects that were hatching, the trout took it with utter abandon. For two hours I had been fast to fish, some of them heavy enough to really work my light rod. Saving only enough to fill the frying pan, I had carefully released all the rest. Now I was sated with fishing, drowsy with the heat and satisfied to just sit and watch the lake and the surrounding slopes.

Apart from the busy sandpiper, not a living thing moved. Across the basin on the shady side of a mountain beneath a ragged snowdrift, an elderly mountain billy goat lay on the flat top of a little outcrop projecting from a patch of broken boulders. Like me and every other animal in the basin, he was enjoying the coolness out of

reach of the blazing sun. Overhead the sky was a fault-
less blue, the kind of day when everything warm-blooded
likes to hunt for a bed in the deep shade. Somewhere up
among the terraces and patches of shin-tangle scrub to
my right and a bit behind me were thirty-odd bighorn
sheep—females, lambs and young rams who had all been
out feeding earlier in the morning, but now were so well
hidden that the most careful combing with powerful
binoculars revealed not so much as the tip of a horn.

For a while I dozed flat on my back with my hat over
my face, but then a distant rumble of thunder brought me
wide awake. Towering over the high ridge rimming the
basin to the west, looking hard and white as carved ivory,
a great mass of cloud was riding in on the southwest
wind. As it came the shape of it changed and it seemed
to grow, the underside appearing in dirty greenish black.
It was time for me to be heading for the tent. But then a
flash of lightning struck the ridge top followed instantly
by a great roar of thunder that bounced off the peaks and
sent its echoes rolling down the canyon below, and I
knew there wasn't time. Taking my rod apart, I left my
fish cached under a flat rock at the water's edge and
climbed to a niche under the rim of a low cliff a few
yards above the lake just as the first big rain drops
splashed the rocks. The place was barely big enough to
sit in, but it was enough.

Again the lightning struck the mountain—closer this
time, with an audible snap preceding the almost instant
shattering blast of thunder. The vibration of it seemed
to tear the bottom out of the thunderhead for the rain
came pouring down, streaming off everything, wetting
the herbage and trees, bouncing in a fine spray where it
hit the naked rock. Again and again the lightning played

its hard bright fingers on the high places until it shook the mountains like a barrage of mighty guns. Water sprayed off the forward brim of my hat and my boot toes where they stuck out from under the overhang, but the rest of me was dry.

Then just as quickly as it began the storm was over. The sun came out warm and cheerful as it lit up myriad drops clinging to every grass blade and leaf. Down valley the thunder continued to roll its drums, while the high arches of a double rainbow gleamed in contrast to the dark face of the retreating storm—so close it seemed possible to reach out and finger the brilliant colors.

Getting to my feet, I climbed up to a commanding point of rocks to sit and glass the slopes. A half hour before, the place had looked lifeless, but now it was moving with wild sheep gamboling and feeding on the lush green terraces just under the talus fans at the foot of the cliffs. They were mostly feeding, but the lambs were in a playful mood. About a dozen of these lighthearted young ones were in the company of an old ewe somewhat apart from the rest, a sort of baby-sitter for the bunch, keeping guard while the mothers fed. She was hungry and content to stay in one spot, but the light-footed little bighorns in her charge wanted no part of it. With a rush they left her to run towards the gnarled and weathered trunk of a huge old mountain larch lying dead among the rocks. There they began a sort of follow-the-leader game around and through its great broken branches, bounding ecstatically back and forth across the big trunk. The nurse ewe climbed slowly towards them, but she had scarcely arrived when they left her again to go at a high gallop down towards a big boulder on a bench meadow beyond a little ridge. It lay half buried where it had halted ages before after a dizzy plunge off the cliffs above. It was covered with multi-colored rock lichen and weathered roughly in tiny ledges making footholds for the lambs as they climbed and played over it. After a few minutes their energy seemed to flag and they stopped in various attitudes on this little mountain sticking up among a sea of wildflowers. One lamb saw the ewe coming over the swell of ground towards them and bleated. She answered and so did its mother from farther down the slope, signals that seemingly reminded all the young ones that they were hungry; for they all began trotting back towards the main bunch bleating as they went.

As each lamb reached its mother, it began to suckle vigorously, each tiny tail wiggling furiously in enthusiastic spurts of movement along with impatient bunting. The feeding was not prolonged. The ewes stood patiently while the pressure of accumulated milk was eased off their udders and they terminated the suckling by simply lifting a hind foot over the necks of their lambs, pushing them away as they stepped ahead.

Now the lambs were scattered through the herd, but before long they were collected again napping in the warm sun in beds up to their ears in brilliant blooms of monkey flowers, paintbrush, heliotrope and many others. Their bedground was amongst a scattering of great, wide-branched larches in lightly dappled shade where the sun filtered down through the feathery green foliage. The breeze was cool now and the sheep were content.

When the binoculars swung back towards the old billy's hanging bedground across the basin, it was to find him feeding in a little pocket five hundred feet farther up among the sheer cliffs. The place was barely big enough to accommodate his angular frame as he stood on the edge of nothing, cropping busily on the lush green stuff growing where a little seep came out of a crack in the rock wall. The freezing and thawing of this water over countless seasons had eroded away the rock, forming a small pocket lined with a thin layer of soil sufficient to support the plant life growing there—mostly goat sorrel along with a thin scattering of fine tufted grass.

It did not take the billy long to get what was readily available, whereupon he moved casually on up the cliff face along a steeply inclining ledge, little more than a figment of imagination from where I sat. Short in the cannon bones, he could reach up and ahead for favorable places to put his hoofs and then lift himself with ease. Like all his kind, the slab-sided shape of his body with narrow hips and shoulders allowed easy passage close to the rock wall in places where a bighorn ram's roundness and thickness of horns and quarters would have pushed him off into space. As goats always do in very steep going unless alarmed, this one climbed with a phlegmatic deliberation, very casual, yet placing each foot with the exactness of a real specialist.

And specialists they are in their own way, as are all animals to one degree or another. But this specialization is more noticeable among goats, for they choose to live, summer and winter, among high crags and cliff faces, rarely coming to lower ground except to cross over between the mountain ranges. Except for some occasional licking at some mineral spring below timberline they stay among the crags. Their trails follow the broken ledges overlooking eagle thoroughfares where not even wolves, coyotes or cougars often venture to challenge their mastery of mountains.

The billy was climbing steadily in the field of my glasses, pulled in close by the magnification in sharp contrast to the dark-colored rock face behind, when an eagle suddenly appeared from somewhere up in the blue vault above like a falling javelin straight at him. The goat must have heard the roar of the wind in its pinion feathers, for it was his leap ahead towards a split in the rock that drew my attention to the eagle. He barely made it to the break where he had room to tuck in his hind quarters when the eagle struck at him. Facing out with his neck bowed, the billy parried with needle-sharp horns forcing the big bird to veer off. The eagle let its momentum carry it up a hundred feet or so, rolled over and struck again, but again the goat bucked on his front feet with a lightning last thrust and once more the reaching talons missed. The eagle struck three times in almost as many seconds, but it had no chance in such a place, so it swooped away to leave the billy alone.

Here was another kind of specialist, not only as a species but as an individual, for comparatively few golden eagles will try to kill a fully grown mountain goat. Once years before, away down amongst the high mountains of Idaho along the Salmon River, I had witnessed a similar attack. I was fishing directly across the Middle Fork from a sheer granite face about fifteen hundred feet high, when a big old billy appeared climbing laterally along a tiny ledge perhaps a hundred feet down from the top. The eagle came from somewhere thousands of feet above in a sizzling dive with the wind a rising crescendo in its wing feathers. The goat likely heard the bird coming before he saw it, for he made about three quick jumps to a spot where a little chimney gave him room to turn and fight. Here with his long chin whisker flying like a banner of defiance he met the eagle in a short fierce battle where no contact was made, though the intent was obvious. Had the eagle reached him two seconds sooner, the goat would have undoubtedly been knocked off the ledge to a certain death on the jagged rocks far below—a well-pulped feed for the big winged predator.

It is not a common thing to observe, for having watched eagles in the vicinity of goats and sheep for un-counted hours over the years, I would say that very few individuals learn how to kill in this fashion. But seeing such a conflict between the winged and four-footed ones makes it apparent that such attacks are successful often enough to be encouraging. This one had failed and now the billy was climbing again in his normal easygoing way, the incident forgotten.

The swinging glasses picked up the eagle and its mate riding a thermal high against the blue sky, circling on motionless outspread wings in a climbing spiral till almost lost from view. Somewhere beneath, hidden among the pinnacles and shelves of the mountain was a nest, but the fledglings therein would have to do with something other than goat this day.

The glasses continued their roving, pausing here and there to examine things that looked like animals but turned out to be something else. Then away up on the skyline to the west of the basin, from the direction the thunderstorm had come, black silhouettes appeared against the sky, the unmistakable shapes of bighorn rams. They were coming up onto the ridge crest from the far side, stopping one by one to look down towards me. There were ten of them in line, all mature animals but one; a fine bachelor's club, veterans of many seasons

with only a single three or four year old among them—a
prince consort among kings. Although they were a long
way off, there was no mistaking the full curled horns.

There are no animals in the mountains more dramatic. For these fit with the big sky and the rugged peaks
of the Rockies, where clouds sail on the wings of the wind
with shadows trailing swiftly below across hanging
meadows, the open talus fans and the heavily timbered
valleys. They live with the song of the wind in their ears,
sometimes a soft caress of sound among rock spires and
weather-bent timberline trees, sometimes a roaring full-
throated crescendo; the background lyrics of wild sheep
country. The two go together like northland lakes and
loons, for one cannot really live without the other; it is
the wind that whips the snow off the flanks and crests of
the wintering grounds allowing the sheep to feed when
the rest of the country is buried deep beneath the cover
of the cold white blanket. The sound of it in summer is a
reminder that one travels in sheep country, even though
these animals may be out of sight.

For a few minutes the rams stood motionless and
then as though at a signal they all trailed the big leader
at a tearing gallop down over a series of broken ledges
and cliffs. One moment they were coming head-on and
the next they had swapped ends in complete reverse to
go streaking back towards the top. Without slacking
stride they turned again to come galloping recklessly
down over a near-impossible place, sure on their nimble
feet, rhythmic as dancers; the lighthearted play of these
four-footed mountaineers. When they came to the top of
an almost perpendicular snowdrift they did not check
their headlong rush, but came down in a bounding glissade with slush flying from their hoofs high over their

backs in glistening showers. They ran out on the top of a big talus fan, stopping there to gaze down over the hanging meadows below and then making their way sedately down to the first green growth as though something as undignified as play was completely beyond consideration.

Fascinated as always with these curly-horned ones, I recalled another day in early May high on the slopes of Sheep Mountain above Kluane Lake in southwestern Yukon Territory. It was a brilliant morning with a vast sweep of mountains spread out beyond the still-frozen expanse of the lake. Perhaps four miles away there was a steep bluff dropping down to the far shore. It looked as though a giant snowball had been smashed against it, for shelves and cliffs were smeared with white. But the whiteness was Dall sheep. My binoculars were not nearly strong enough to make a count, but there must have been close to three hundred head in the bunch.

Directly in front of me, scattered in bunches for three-quarters of a mile, there were close to a hundred more, mostly ewes, new lambs and yearlings. Not all the ewes had lambs with them yet, for the lambing season had just begun. Not more than a hundred and fifty yards away, up at the foot of a broken cliff, five big herdmasters were loafing in the sun. Two of them were fine old rams with magnificent flaring horns, the tips perfect. They were paying me the compliment of ignoring me completely, although my perch was in plain view.

I wanted to get to the top of that cliff, for above it was a tableland of tundra, where there were likely more sheep, but I was not sure where to tackle it. Wondering if the rams would show the way, I climbed slowly towards them until barely fifty feet separated us. They stood bunched up gazing curiously at me, and then one of the lesser ones nudged the old leader gently on the flank with a horn tip as though prompting him to move. He took the cue and in a very deliberate and dignified way led the bunch up along the foot of the cliff to a break and climbed up onto the shelves with me trailing along at a respectful hundred feet behind. Then, he showed us all a route up the rock face that was so easy I could have climbed it with both hands in my pockets. When we reached the top they left me at a tearing gallop as though suddenly tired of my intrusion and wishing to be left alone.

From the mountains on the coast of Alaska to the Mackenzie Range to the east, and from the north slope of the Brooks Range south to the peaks within sight of the great Peace River, these northern thinhorn sheep, *Ovis dalli dalli* and *Ovis dalli stonei*, flourish. They go from snowy white in Alaska and western Yukon to almost black in certain individuals found among the mountains on the headwaters of the Halfway, Musqua, Prophet and Prairie rivers. In between they run in every shade of grey. Some, like those found in the Snyder Mountains north of the Nahanni River, have black tails and black stripes on their shins. The so-called Fannin sheep, with their blue-grey saddles, listed as a separate species by the early biological "splitters," are truly just another color phase of Dall sheep. You can sit on a slope up near Teslin Lake near the Yukon–British Columbia border and see wild sheep that range from the next thing to pure white to iron blue in color, all grazing on the same slopes and certainly all interbreeding.

The Peace River seems to have formed an effective fence that has kept the thinhorns and bighorns from mingling, for they likely would freely interbreed if they came together. There is a gap of about one hundred and fifty miles across where there are no sheep. South of the river and a bit east of Pine Pass is the northern limit of bighorn range. From there these are found all along the Rockies away south to the mountains of Sonora and Baiha in old Mexico. Over this vast reach of country the bighorn family tree divides itself into three main branches: *Ovis canadensis canadensis*, the Canada bighorn; *Ovis canadensis californi*, the California bighorn; and *Ovis canadensis nelsoni*, the desert bighorn. The California bighorn is found as far west as the Okanagin and Fraser Valleys as well as in Washington State.

From the far north, where the winter night is six months long, and the mountains are whipped mercilessly by howling blizzards with a wind chill reaching an equivalent of one hundred fifty degrees below zero, to far south in the dry and equally merciless heat of the desert mountains, the wild sheep have adapted themselves remarkably well to the wide range of conditions they face. Only the grizzly bear matches their ability to adapt to climate, but is not nearly so successful at meeting the pressures of men. The wild sheep have certainly suffered from human encroachment and much of their former ranges are no longer populated; but they still survive—often in good numbers where the country provides adequate shelter and feed.

Wonderfully intelligent, blithe creature that it is, the mountain sheep is the hallmark of the remaining mountain habitat in western North America; the one animal completely synonymous with the high rugged ranges—the land of the sky.

2

Hoofs and Horns in High Country

Many years ago when still a small boy, I was fishing one day in a favorite place along Drywood Creek where it poured down over a series of water-smoothed shelves at the bottom of a narrow canyon. The valley floor through which this canyon was cut had been scoured out between the mountains by ancient ice; the features of it giving away its origin for it was U-shaped in cross section. But the canyon had been carved by the creek over the thousands of years since the ice had retreated, and by contrast it was narrower at the top in certain spots than it was at the bottom. There were places where one could stand looking up at shelves stacked in reverse in a series of overhangs completely impossible for a bighorn or even a goat to climb. Goats never came to this place, but the wild sheep did on occasion in the heat of summer, and their route of descent the last one hundred fifty feet into the canyon was where a branch creek, dry except in spring, had cut a blind gulch into it from the side.

There on a small bar of fine sand and gravel at its mouth, I had seen their tracks on occasion, a discovery that mystified me for some time because for the life of me, I could not understand how they got down the walls of that narrow cleft, really little more than a large crack in the rock from ten to fifteen feet across. What few ledges there were on each side were insignificant and far enough apart to appear utterly impossible. The inner end was as smooth as only water-worn rock can be and the next thing to straight up. It was completely unclimbable for anything but a fly and that would have to be an extremely persistent and long-winded insect. I was more than mystified, I was baffled and curious as well, for unquestionably the sheep used this place to get up and down into the canyon. Looking at it closely one day after finding some fresh ram tracks at the bottom, the somewhat facetious thought struck me that they must have somehow learned to fly. Strangely enough, this seemingly ridiculous idea was close to being right.

There was a big pool at the foot of the falls on the main creek just above the mouth of the ravine. It was as far upstream as trout could go, for the creek poured over a projecting ledge like the lip of a jug in a sheer plunge fifteen or twenty feet into the deep pool below. It was a favorite place of mine, cool even in the hottest days of summer, for the creek played curtains of spray on the canyon walls all along a series of falls farther up the canyon, leaping and jumping down over water-worn ledges and chutes, shaking itself and gamboling in utter abandon as it roared and chuckled from pool to pool. The big pool at the bottom always contained trout and these were an added attraction to the place.

One hot afternoon I was coming up the creek heading

for this spot partially screened by a big boulder a few yards below the mouth of the side gulch, when the sight of a bunch of big rams froze me in my tracks. There were six of them standing in various attitudes on the edge of the pool where they had been drinking, for droplets of water were still falling from one ram's muzzle as it turned its head toward me. They had seen me about the same instant I had seen them and for a few long moments joined me in a tableau of mutual surprise framed in the red and green argyllite of the canyon walls, with the backdrop of the falls beyond.

Then, as one, they wheeled to leap toward the mouth of the ravine. Bounding in pursuit as fast as my feet could carry me, I came into the end of the ravine to see a wonderful sight. The rams were not climbing at a run but were literally flying with the sheerest kind of daring and sure-footed grace. Instead of going up one side of the rift, they were leaping from ledge to ledge back and forth across it, and it was perfectly apparent that they were not strangers to this place, for nowhere did they hesitate an instant.

The big leader with a massive set of horns was pointing the way as they threaded back and forth in a marvelous pattern of running, climbing and leaping, taking them up towards the rim like a well-ordered and practiced team of gymnasts. Never before or since have I seen such a magnificent display of sure-footed, utterly wild, yet superbly precise exhibition of fast climbing. It was more than climbing in places, for the rams leapt across and up the chasm catching a narrow ledge, and by daring use of their momentum and exact knowledge of the next foothold, leapt back and across to the next. There perhaps they could run and climb a ways before again taking to the air. In a few seconds they had reached the rim and were gone. Behind them, all that remained to mark their passage was a puff of dust lit up in a shaft of sunlight against the blue sky.

While wild sheep cannot begin to follow mountain goats out across sheer cliffs, in more broken going among chimneys, turrets and natural buttresses, where there is room to clear their width of horns and bodies, there are no more superb climbers in the world. They are very strong, light-footed and quick. Not only do they plant their feet fast and firmly with confidence where a goat would go with deliberation and care, but they do so at a dead run making use of a combination of balance and momentum to carry them across places seemingly utterly impossible to traverse. They have a wonderful sense of rhythm. In view of the fact that a big ram's head can weigh up to fifty pounds or more, their climbing ability is more than amazing, it is outright defiance of gravity.

Universally, throughout their ranges, the mountain sheep spend their lives wandering mountain slopes tempering themselves with climbing, and they are well designed for it. Their legs are trim, but there is nothing fragile about them, for they are flat-boned, strong and well designed for the use put to them. They are short-coupled and muscular, thick in the shoulders and haunches, with well-sprung ribs and muscular loins and necks.

As an old mountain man put it one day while we sat our horses watching a bunch of startled bighorns crossing a field of broken boulders at a tearing gallop with all the ease they might show on a well-groomed lawn: "Wish I could find a horse that could go like that! It would sure save a heap of riding around patches of this country that gets in the way. Those sons-o-guns go on a run where a man would be scared to walk, and then turn on a dime and give you some change!"

On northern ranges, the winter coat of wild sheep is one of nature's most refined examples of what amounts to perfect insulation. The outer guard hairs are thick and hollow like those of the deer family, each hair being a tube with dead air inside. This by itself is an excellent shield against the cold, but is further reinforced by a heavy underlayer of fine wool. The combination makes a wind- and frostproof covering from one to four inches deep, real armor against the cold.

Only the mountain goat's thick white covering of wool and hair surpasses it among the mountain animals of North America.

Many times in winter when temperatures are sub-zero with a strong wind blowing among the peaks in back of our ranch, the deer and elk will be taking shelter in timber or under the lee of bluffs, but the bighorns will be out in the open feeding and bedding down where the chill factor is way below zero. I have been aloft with them on days like this, when it was sheer torture in spite of the best of winter clothing; but the sheep would be happily going about their activities as though a chinook was blowing.

Climbing with the wild sheep in winter is more than uncomfortable, it can be dangerous—for they traverse with complete nonchalance places where the rock and hard drifts are rimmed with a coating of frost or a layer of hard ice. Their squarish hoofs are shaped to grip such surfaces like suction cups in places where a man must exercise extreme caution to avoid a fall that could be fatal.

Avalanches are another hazard that can trap the unwary, but if one watches the sheep and follows their lead, there is not much danger of being caught in a snowslide. For all wild sheep of the northern mountains have an un-canny sense of such danger, and will avoid places where an avalanche can be triggered. If a man takes the time to study their choice of routes he can climb through country ripe with hanging snow, but it may mean taking circu-itous routes around places that may look like easy short cuts. Wild sheep almost never get caught in avalanches.

As has been pointed out, their choice of some ranges in the far north involves country little short of impossible for a man to survive in during the long winter, when the sun is gone except for a glow on the southern horizon at midday. The sheep endure and survive in conditions dif-ficult to describe. Charles Sheldon recounts some rare days of endurance while he was collecting specimens of Dall sheep in the mountains overlooking the Toklat and East Fork rivers early in this century. On what were comparatively mild days for that region, he encountered cold and wind conditions where an accident could spell death by freezing in a few hours.

Sometimes in bighorn country the winter winds can be a real hazard even when warm, as I found out one day on the south face of The Horn overlooking Trail Creek and Horseshoe Canyon.

It was a fairly warm day in January with a mild chinook wind blowing, when I spotted a bunch of rams feeding amongst a dozen bull elk up on a grassy wind-swept saddle fifteen hundred feet above the canyon floor. Wanting some film illustrating this competition for win-ter feed, I began climbing towards them. It is necessary to understand something of chinook winds to appreciate what happened next.

In this region the prevailing winds are from the southwest, originating away out over the Pacific Ocean— waters warmed by the Japanese current. Because they are warm these air currents rise to high altitudes, drifting northeasterly towards British Columbia. Over the mountains inland, they begin to cool, lose altitude as a result and speed up. Upon striking the main chain of the Rockies which form the backbone of the continent, they bounce exactly like fast water striking sunken rocks to form a standing wave that may reach along the mountain front for two or three hundred miles. As these air currents plunge, the friction set up by the peaks and the turbulence tends to warm them, and at the top of the standing wave, where a cold layer of upper air is often encountered, there forms a long line of black clouds. With a strip of clear blue sky between it and the mountains, this is the famous chinook arch. Such a chinook wind can raise the temperature as much as sixty to one hundred degrees within an hour or two in winter. It can reach a velocity of well over one hundred miles per hour, and can whip the snow off vast areas of range in a very short time. Thus it is a blessing in deep snow country for all grazing wildlife as well as the cattle ranchers—but also unpredictable, as I was about to find out this day.

For a while, as I climbed, the bulge of the mountain hid me from the sheep and elk, but when I came to a level where the bench could be seen, they had disappeared. It was unlikely they had seen me or smelled me, so I kept going, expecting to find them in a dip beyond the bench. But when I was only a few steps from the top of the shoulder, I suddenly walked into a wind stream that slammed into me with such fierceness it took my breath away. It grabbed me and twisted like nothing ever experienced, knocked me off balance and then blasted me off the end of the bluff. By nothing but sheer luck, it propelled me squarely into a big gnarled old pine growing out of a ledge below with its roots firmly anchored in solid rock. Somewhere I had dropped my tripod, but my camera was safe in my pack. It was a bit unnerving to find myself draped like a dish rag on my belly over a stout limb, completely unable to move, looking helplessly down at jagged rocks a hundred feet below. Wondering what next, I could only wait for a lull in the wind, and when it came it gave me time to get down to earth and flatten out. Between gusts I crawled back, found my tripod and proceeded on hands and knees back down the slope.

Sometimes the wind forced me to lie flat hanging onto anything near enough to grab with eyes tight shut, my face stung by bits of flying grass and rock. In this fashion I crawled and squirmed two hundred yards down my backtrail to the shelter of some timber on the lee side of a little hogback ridge. By this time I was about exhausted, feeling beat up and sore all over. But apart from a nasty bruise on my ribs donated by the lifesaving limb on the tree, and a painfully skinned wrist, I was all right. Where the sheep and elk had gone, I had no idea, and right then could not have cared less.

More than one sheep hunter has found himself in danger from the force of wind. I recall another time when Bert Riggall, a hunter, and I were climbing the lee side of a peak while the wind slated and banged at skyline two thousand feet over our heads. Where we were it was practically windless. I heard something buzz and the sound seemed to come from directly overhead. Our hunter noticed it too, and mentioned something about it being a queer thing to hear bees in a place like that. Bert's hearing was none too good, but he lifted the earflaps on his cap and listened. A few seconds later we heard the sound again.

"Bees, hell!" he exclaimed. "That's rocks! Let's get out of here!"

It was flat pieces of shale being blown off the ridge above and planing down past us so fast they were hard to see. If one had struck a man, it could have flattened his head. It was a salutary lesson in what wind can do, and one never forgotten.

More than one man has been severely injured by wind when sheep hunting. When I was a boy I recall a young man who was blown off a ledge by a sudden gust of wind and fell down a dozen feet into jagged rocks, breaking his arm. He was alone and miles from home, but he managed to get back to his horse. Suffering greatly from pain and shock, he was almost unconscious when he reached help.

When winter winds have subsided and the temperature climbs in spring, one finds the sheep low on the flanks of the mountains and feeding on the first green growth on slopes facing the sun. At this time of year the bighorns in my back yard suffer from the heat of their heavy coats and also from ticks.

For the Rocky Mountain spotted fever tick abounds in these mountains in spring, and while not infected with spotted fever here, this bloodsucking, very bothersome insect can make life miserable for man or beast. No other insect can be such a particular kind of pest, for this one buries its head into its host, hanging onto the flesh with mandibles like tiny hooks, filling up on blood till it swells from the size of a small apple seed into the proportions of a grape. Then it releases its hold and falls off onto the ground to procreate its species. Whatever animal it bites knows the feeling of interminable itching that can last long after the tick is gone, especially if it is knocked off before it is ready to leave, for then its mandibles are left behind to set up an infection and itching that can continue for weeks. When it is springtime in the Rockies the stanzas of the song proclaim romance and beauty, but there is more to it than that where ticks are concerned. Certainly everything warm-blooded is aware of them.

One time while stalking a bunch of ewes and rams on a hot day in April, I came up to them at close range, but found them all lying down chewing their cuds and panting from the heat. Naturally I was delighted to be practically mingling with them and totally ignored, but their lack of activity left something to be desired where motion picture film was concerned.

Standing there behind my tripod wondering how long it would be before they decided to move, I absent-mindedly scratched a tick bite. A two year old ram was watching me intently; my scratching had caught his attention. I exaggerated the scratching a bit and in a few minutes every sheep in the bunch had its eyes fastened on me. Then the power of suggestion got hold of them. First they began shaking their heads and batting their ears back and forth. Then one by one they got up to rub themselves vigorously on rocks and scrub trees, kicking at the backs of their ears, and generally behaving as though attacked by every tick on the mountain at once. It was a comical thing to watch and an interesting sequence to put on film. Several times since, I have worked this trick, and it never fails to catch on.

The Rocky Mountain spotted fever tick has probably been researched more than any other insect, and it is

doubtful if the recounting of this experience adds much
to the mysteries that still surround it. However, we know
that when these insects are active, they sometimes swarm
on a weakened animal sucking its blood, infecting it and
on occasion causing a kind of paralysis, sometimes ending in death. Ticks are found in a large portion of the
bighorn ranges, but there are none in the Dall sheep
mountains to the north.

The senses of the mountain sheep are almost identi-
cally developed from one extreme limit of their range to
the other. Indeed, from the accounts of James L. Clark in
his very comprehensive book, *The Great Arc of the Wild
Sheep*, and from what has been said by hunters like Warren Page, Jack O'Connor and others who have hunted
widely, there are not many differences found throughout
the world.

Ernest Thomson Seton quotes an Indian hunter as
having said: "Bighorn can't hear thunder, can't smell
dead horse, but can see through rock!" While this state-
ment is relatively correct where comparison of seeing and
hearing are concerned, they do have fair noses. By way
of interesting comparison, the senses of mountain goats
are about parallel, although their reactions to messages
thus received are a great deal more phlegmatic.

Such famous sheep hunters, observers and scribes as
Charles Sheldon, James L. Clark, Jack O'Connor, Warren Page, Bert Riggall, and Jimmy Simpson universally
agree that wild sheep have good noses and use them
with considerable success for protection. Charles Sheldon,
in his voluminous accounts of incidents in the Yukon
and Alaska during his extensive expeditions after Dall
sheep early in this century, cites many instances when
the quarry got his scent and departed hastily to safer

places. However, I disagree with him when he attributes this to an inherent fear of man even where man
has not been encountered before. I do not believe that
animals which have never known man are born with an
unreasoning fear of him; it is something they acquire
through experience, the reactions of their mothers and
observation of other species around them. I am convinced
that man smells very bad to most animals, particularly so
when he has been camping out at timberline for weeks,
sweating like a horse from climbing steep country, and
going without a bath because he dislikes ice cold water.
Their wish to leave upon smelling him stems from sheer
desire for comfort more than fear. However, a hunter,
through extrasensory perception or whatever you wish to
call it, does telegraph his intentions no matter whether he
wears two legs or four, or which direction the wind is
blowing—a fact that very few observers recognize.

One time during a prolonged effort at capturing bighorns on film, I had a salutary experience illustrating
their reaction to human smell.

From across a steep canyon at a range of nearly half a
mile I spotted a big ram I knew very well from many previous encounters. He was bedded on a shelf near the top
of the opposite rim in a very spectacular place, where a
fine sequence could be added to my stock of film if it
could be taken from the right angle. Watching him
through my glasses, I was sure he was watching me—
exactly what was wanted, for my technique revolves on
the principle of completely peaceful, straightforward association with very rarely any attempt being made to approach under cover.

However, it would be necessary for me to be out of
this ram's sight for a considerable distance while climb-

ing to his level from below. In order to keep him posted as to my whereabouts, I planned to give him my wind all the way. It was my hope that by doing this, my scent would be at first well diluted by distance but grow stronger gradually as I approached and thus would not cause him to move. This and the fact that it was a balmy, lazy kind of morning might work in my favor.

My route of stalk was directly down and up a very precipitous piece of mountain and took longer than planned, for I was carrying twenty-odd pounds of camera and tripod on my shoulder. Balancing it and avoiding bumping it on rocks, at the same time sticking to the faces along my route, slowed me up. But finally, as I slowly and deliberately came up over a ledge not twenty feet in front of the ram, it was to see him still bedded down and obviously unafraid, though his eyes widened at the sight of me and very obviously he was not enjoying my smell. He wrinkled his nose and elevated his upper lip in the most comical expression of sheer disgust ever seen on a ram's face. Then he got to his feet with a long and extremely suggestive sniff to walk away along the ledge to a spot where the wind was sweet and came to a stand to look me over some more. I got his picture there but unfortunately missed his first reaction; a great shame, for it illustrated something long suspected.

Many times over the years while fraternizing with wild sheep at very close range and being accepted by them as just another animated and harmless part of life on their mountains, I have noted their discomfort when my position was directly upwind. It takes considerable close association before they become sufficiently accustomed to what must be a very disagreeable odor to the point of ignoring it.

When I read an account of how a hunter froze in his tracks during a stalk when a rock was accidentally dislodged to go clattering down a steep slope, I know he does not know wild sheep very well. For unless the quarry is in sight, such concern is unnecessary. Short of some alien sound like the clink of metal or the prolonged unbroken crunching of human steps on crusted snow or loose shale, they pay small attention to their ears as a means of defense. The mountains are full of noise: the wind roaring and banging through chimneys, brush and trees; the clatter of rocks falling off high faces onto the talus fans; the distant thunder of ice falls or storms all add up to a great deal of sound. If they paid attention to everything they hear they would be in a constant state of nervous turmoil. Hence their ears are in no way as keen as those of the deer.

On many occasions grizzlies have been seen digging for ground squirrels or marmots directly above a band of sheep. This big furry mountaineer is a most enthusiastic excavator who thinks nothing of heaving big rocks out of his way, which go leaping and bounding down the slopes below with noises like gun shots. Such a bear can be located at long range sometimes by the intermittent booming and crashing of falling rock. When sheep find themselves in line with such a bombardment, they show little concern other than moving casually to the side where they go back to feeding or loafing with practically no other acknowledgment of the source of the disturbance.

Sheep do use their ears, however, for audio-communication between bands or individuals. There is always considerable blatting going on between mothers and lambs. They keep in touch with each other, signifying their location and wants by such signals. The rams call to each other and to the ewes during breeding season on occasion with a hoarse bah-ah-ah. More than once I have had one look down at me off a rim and give this guttural call.

While development of their ears is mediocre, their eyes are marvelously keen and the main means of protection from enemies. It is estimated that they can see as well as a man aided by a pair of the very best eight-power binoculars.

Once I was sitting watching a ram lying half asleep on a ledge a few steps above me among some broken rock ledges. He was absentmindedly chewing his cud, when suddenly he swallowed it and came to his feet to gaze fixedly away out across the valley past me towards a hanging basin on the face of a peak at least a mile away. Although my vision is excellent, I could see nothing of what had caught his attention until I screwed the focus of my nine-power glasses down sharp and fine. Then the heliographing flashes of white rump patches in the sun gave away the location of a bunch of young rams running and playing on some open, broken scree. After watching intently for a few moments, the big ram beside me was apparently satisfied with what he saw, for he turned away to begin cropping herbage, completely relaxed. He had read the message, and it said no danger was involved with the action.

Like the white-tail deer's wig-wagging flag and the very specialized expanding white rump ruff of the prairie pronghorn antelope, the rump patch of the bighorn and stone sheep offers an easily seen means of visual communication at very long range. It is thus the approach of danger or another band is telegraphed. When man used mirrors to heliograph messages before the advent of wireless, telephones and radio, he was borrowing a natural endowment from the four-footed ones.

While Seton's Indian may have exaggerated a bit when he claimed wild sheep could see through rock, there was no doubting some experiences in his recall, as in mine, when such sheer magic was suspected. For, along with the eyes of mountain goats, antelopes, eagles, hawks, owls and vultures, the eyes of the wild sheep are among the keenest found in all nature.

Like most animals, mountain sheep have a kind of extrasensory perception telling them at a distance if a predator, be it coyote, wolf or man, is hungry and hunting or just passing through. Many times I have seen coyotes in the vicinity of sheep and if the little grey wolf is mousing or just going some place, they pay little more than passing attention. But let one show up with mutton in mind and every eye will be riveted on him, even though said coyote may be putting on a sham as if such a thing could not be farther from his intentions.

If a man shows up carrying a rifle, gumshoeing from one bit of cover to another, intent on collecting a ram, these animals can interpret his intentions at great distances and make themselves amongst the hardest quarry in the world to approach. At first, the photographer that shows up in high pastures will be regarded with not a little suspicion, but his attitude and frame of mind are far different from those of the rifle hunter. If he is patient and knows something of these wild ones, it will not be too long before he is tolerated at very close range under something like normal circumstances.

For reasons of protection the mountain sheep prefers to live on high steep ground. Even when following local migration routes between summering and wintering country, they always follow ridges if the topography of the ground allows. But they do on occasion cross low ground to reach an objective. Sometimes in the north and in the desert this may mean a considerable distance.

Jack O'Connor, well-known gun editor of *Outdoor Life* magazine, tells of seeing signs where sheep have crossed miles of flat desert between mountain ranges. He suspects they observe a storm dumping rain on distant country, or maybe smell the moisture on the wind, and will traverse considerable distances to reach the place knowing that there will be lush new growth and replenished water holes.

Once when traveling the narrow winding road through Mount McKinley Park in Alaska, movement of something white caught my attention away out on the brush-grown flats of the Teklaneeka River. The binoculars revealed twenty-two head of Dall sheep—ewes, lambs and yearlings traveling in a string towards the mountains at the head of the river. Their route crossed several miles of low, comparatively flat ground and even at that distance it was easy to note that they were spooked on unfamiliar terrain where they are vulnerable to wolves. They do this every spring and fall, for the well-known biologist Adolph Murie, also observing wildlife in the region that year, told me he had seen sheep away out on these flats several times.

Mountain sheep offer a wonderful challenge to the hunter or nature observer, for apart from their built-in flair for doing things dramatically, the grandeur and magnificent sweeps of country they inhabit are great medicine for a civilization-softened body and a weary soul. For if one lives with these blithe cliffhangers for a while, the problems of the world tend to diminish to true perspective, and one becomes aware that real wealth is health, a strong body, peace of mind and an ability to view things as they really are. What has always amazed me is the wild sheep's adaptability to whatever conditions he encounters, even when these are sometimes engineered by man. Given any kind of break at all and some decent, truly objective management, these mountaineers will always be with us.

For this is a very intelligent animal, a characteristic perhaps best illustrated by their penchant for various kinds of play—some is lighthearted aimless frolic, to be sure, but they also enjoy stylized and organized games.

Bert Riggall and I saw a very interesting and entertaining sight one evening up at Twin Lakes just under the Continental Divide only a few miles north of the extreme southwestern corner of Alberta, where one can put his arm around a boundary monument and be in two provinces of Canada, the State of Montana and two countries all at the same time.

It was the shank of a fine July day, supper was just over, the packtrain horses were turned loose and we were sitting in front of the tents glassing for game, when a bunch of bighorn ewes, lambs and small rams appeared on the skyline. As we watched, a dignified old grandmother ewe ran down the near slope of the ridge top to launch herself down a steeply pitched snowdrift towards the upper lip of a sheer cliff several hundred feet high. She cut loose in a reckless glissade with the icy snow streaming up over both shoulders in showers. She seemed hell-bent to commit suicide; but at the last fraction of a second, she did a kind of four-legged Christy turn off the drift onto the naked rock to head back up the slope at a gallop. Every sheep in the bunch followed her with the same breakneck abandon, each one making that hair-raising turn on the very brink of disaster. Around and around they went for the better part of half an hour playing their version of "Follow the Leader."

They also play a replica of "I'm the King of the Castle." Another time Bert and I saw five young rams playing this game on a loose pile of shale left by a snowslide. One would take position on top of the pile, and the rest took turns trying to dislodge him, while he whirled, danced and parried with his horns knocking back all comers, until finally dislodged. Then the victor took his turn at holding the "castle."

Over the years since then, I have seen this game played several times, once by a quartet of big old bachelor-club herdmasters; craggy, battle-scarred veterans, but lighthearted as lambs in their enjoyment of the game.

Sometimes a game seems to be completely spontaneous though extremely stylized, as my son Dick and I noted one day while trailing a big ram accompanied by four ewes at the tail end of the rutting season.

They were moving out ahead of us up a slightly inclining bench through about eight inches of powder snow, strung out at a walk with the ram in the lead. Suddenly the four ewes exploded into action. Flashing out in a fast run like the spokes of a wheel, they went a few quick jumps, and then, in perfect unison, they jumped straight up, swapped ends and came back to a common center. Just a jump from a four-way, head-on collision, they reared and propelled themselves straight up again with a powerful thrust of hind legs, turning again in mid-air to face out and go out on the original pattern. Their timing was perfect—so perfect one could set music to it. They repeated this wild quadrille several times, then as though at a signal they suddenly quit, to fall in sedately behind the ram once more as though such frivolous doings were utterly beyond their dignity. This was the only time over years of observing that we saw them do this routine.

Quite often in observing nature one sees a group of animals, birds or insects doing something in play or mating ritual that is so marvelously timed and stylish, it is almost possible to hear the undertones of music in the background. The wild sheep are not alone in this by any means, for it is something practiced by many associated species, including man.

Indeed it is obvious to anyone who has ever seen it, that the Prairie Chicken Dance of the Blackfeet Indians was copied even to costume, drum and music from the sharptail and pinnated grouse, the mating dance of the cocks.

I once filmed a marvelous sequence of six or eight small, highly colored butterflies apparently licking salt at a sheep lick in the mountains. They were all going through a highly stylized routine as they picked up salt off the surface of a flat rock, a minuet of exquisite motion accompanied by graceful waving of wings, all carried out in absolutely perfect unison. Watching them on the face of the dark red rock, one was not required to exercise much imagination to hear music by Strauss or one of his contemporaries in the background—the softly singing strings of muted violins, piano and other instruments.

One of the most dramatic sights in the Rocky Mountains is a fight between two mighty bighorn rams, and this too can be almost perfectly timed. When he made his film *The Vanishing Prairie*, Walt Disney was moved to accompany fighting rams with an excerpt from the Anvil Chorus. It fitted beautifully, even though it did jar one's sensibilities a bit by being overbearing.

When two rams square off to fight over dominance of the females during breeding season on a frosty morning and the mountains wake to the ringing crash of horns, it is a time for the gods to stand and watch. It is not like the earth-shaking brawling between two massive buffalo bulls, where main strength and an ability to take punishment name the victor. Nor does it resemble the profane, pounding, chewing, knock-down-and-drag-out fighting of grizzlies. It is a duel of champions with great curling horns for weapons, and the timing of the head-on, midair collisions is usually so precise as to be within half an inch of absolute zero.

And, strangely enough, the victor sometimes misses the reward for his efforts, for upon the first collision, when the banging of horns wakes the echoes, any young four or five year old ram in the vicinity is instantly triggered into a run to investigate. His interest is not that of a spectator, but the ewe in oestrus causing the fight; and while the big ones are trying to loosen each other's brains, the young swift one steals the prize away. It is pure drama set among the snow-draped peaks. I have seen it set to accompaniment of wind howling among the chimneys and turrets of the mountain faces, while snow devils spun and danced like ghostly dervishes all around—backlit by the weak sun of winter.

The copulation of wild sheep is preceded by much maneuvering and display. When several rams are present, the gradience of dominance between them is not all established by fighting. For the bigger rams take the lead by showing off superior physical attributes for the benefit of all concerned. The dominating ram extends his nose straight out, laying his horns down close on each side of his neck and then walks toward a rival or a ewe nudging with his nose or sometimes striking with a hoof to punctuate his presence. Upon coming to a stop, he will tip his head one way or another to display his magnificent and impressive weapons to fullest advantage, thus making his point: he is the big chief, the most fearsome fighter, and will stand for no nonsense. Quite often the competition for dominance goes no farther than this sparring, occasionally accompanied by shouldering and crossing of necks. But when an equally big ram is present, not impressed with an adversary's display, there will be a fight, and it is then the mountains ring with the impact of horns meeting with the flat crack of two heavy hardwood mallets swung together.

At such times the ewes get rough treatment, for if a ewe is not quite ready and tries to run away, she is instantly pursued by every ram in sight. I once saw a ewe take refuge on a cliff, where two rams courting her dared not come close, for to do so would have put one at the mercy of the other where a fall would be fatal. I crept close to film this dramatic impasse and was completely ignored by the rams. But the ewe got nervous and made a break for the top of the rim a dozen feet or so over her head. Instantly both rams were in hot pursuit and at the top were joined by four more—all big mature individuals.

The mountain flattened out here into a gently sloping plateau with the spine of a rock rib running down its center. The ewe led the procession up one side of this rib for two hundred yards, then crossed it to come tearing down the other side. As she spun around the near tip of the rib, I was standing with tripod planted just inside her circle. As she made her turn she was not a dozen feet from me and every ram skidded in her tracks with hoofs throwing dirt up on the surface of the snow. The last one cut the bend on the inside and I barely sidestepped in time to

avoid being run over! I could easily have poked him with
a tripod leg as he shot by.

Then a young, fleetfooted four year old came out of
nowhere from the flank to cut the ewe away down the
mountain slope. The older rams with their heavy horns
were no match for him, and one by one they dropped out
of the race. A half hour later I witnessed the mating of
the younger ram and the ewe—a copulation that is swift
and decisive and may be repeated several times by various
rams in the course of peak oestrus.

Sometimes the fighting between rams during the rut
takes place high up on some shelf on a cliff face, where a
slip on ice-covered rock means sure death for the unfortunate one. I once found the skull of a magnificent ram
lying at the foot of a cliff amongst spring flowers, but no
other bones. Curious, I shed my pack and climbed the
face. On almost every ledge to a point two-thirds of the
way to the top, I picked up various parts of the ram's
skeleton. Most of the bones were on a broad shelf a hundred sheer feet from the upper rim. Had he been knocked
off the top of the cliff in a fight? Or had a cougar killed
him on the ledge? It was something of a mystery, but the
condition of the teeth told me he had been in the prime of
life, and the horn rings said he had been killed in winter.
It was a mystery only the mountain could reveal and it
has not told.

Very few wild sheep ever die peacefully of old age,
for such is the way of nature, especially where the cud-
chewers are concerned. Age and abrasion inevitably
cause the lower jaw's front nipping teeth to drop out,
and thus starvation brought about by an inability to nip
off feed even when belly deep in forage brings the animal
to a cruel and tragic end. Along toward spring and

green-up time, when the physical condition of all grazers is at its lowest ebb and the mountain draws are filled with soft, undermined snow, the old ones often bog down, too weak to help themselves. There coyotes usually find them, and literally eat them alive.

Men prey on sheep too, but the ram that falls to a well-aimed bullet is lucky, for the end of his trail is swift and clean. It is the obligation of all hunters to know their weapons well and make their aim true; for the wild sheep is the grandest game animal of them all.

In spring, when the early wildflowers nod and dance in the breeze and sun, the ewes drop their lambs in suitably secluded lambing grounds with many mothers using the same general area. A little bighorn weighs in the vicinity of five pounds; Dall lambs about a pound less on the average. They are handsome, active little creatures. Unlike the young of most of the deer family, which are wobbly and uncertain on their legs for the first couple of weeks following birth, wild sheep lambs are practically born able to use their running gear to a remarkable degree.

Up near Kluane Lake (pronounced kloo-waw-nee) one spring, I saw a Dall sheep give birth to a lamb years ago. It was not a long, drawn-out process but took only a few minutes. The ewe was located on a ledge up on a rough, broken face, where there was barely room for her to lie down. The lamb got to its feet almost immediately to stand a bit shakily while its mother licked it dry. Then showing very little concern for its safety, she led the way on up the gently inclining ledge with the lamb trailing at her heels. It was still wobbly but rapidly gaining strength. Upon reaching a spot where the ledge widened a bit—something more like the kind of terrain a thoughtful mother would take her newborn for a stroll—the ewe let the lamb suckle. The milk of wild sheep must have wonderful qualities, for when they proceeded, the lamb was skipping and leaping as surefootedly as any such mountain sprite could be.

When a Dall lamb is born of its white mother, it has a bluish grey tint to its coat, which it retains for a few days before turning white. This is not a change of the color of the pelage, but due to a lengthening of the coat covering the black hide showing through when it is born.

Single lambs are generally the rule among mountain sheep, although twins are not unknown. Depending on the quality of range, the ewes nurse them from three to four months before weaning them. In extremely dry desert regions the lactation period may be shortened and then the young ones must feed themselves the best they can manage among sparse growth. As always, life in the wilds is a sort of contest with conditions that is won by the lucky and the fittest. While the ewes are excellent mothers, sometimes their vigilance and knowledge of habitat fail them, and the lamb is lost. Wolves, coyotes, lynx, bobcats, cougars and occasionally eagles take their toll. Even the grizzly has been known to catch a lamb.

In 1963 when we were camped near the Toklat River in Mount McKinley Park, Alaska, we met Adolph Murie one day, and he told us an interesting story.

Earlier that day he had seen a grizzly surprise a band of ewes and lambs in a ravine by coming on them suddenly from directly above at close range. The big animal made a quick dash in amongst them, seized a lamb, killed it, and then ate it on the spot with obvious relish!

Although I have never seen ewes fight another animal,

their short sharp horns are weapons for thrusting, and it is likely that the smaller predators hesitate to tackle them. The big curling horns of the rams are formidable in a different way, but how much they are used against predators is a question.

Certainly against such an animal as a cougar or wolf neither ewes nor rams would have much chance in a close-quarters battle. Two friends of mine, Ernie Haug and Jerry Hadfield, were working on the Red Rock road in Waterton Park one afternoon, when a sudden blatting and rattling of rocks drew their attention up the slope. Down from the foot of some broken cliffs came a big ram in frantic plunges, hoarsely blatting in terror, with a big cougar riding on his back. The ram carried him across the road right in front of their truck and on down the mountain toward the creek. Apparently the cougar had jumped the ram up among the ledges, missed his killing hold and was trying to get it as the terrified sheep tore downhill. A few yards below the road, the cougar pulled the ram down and killed him, after riding the unfortunate animal for close to three hundred yards.

This was a very rare sight for anyone to see, for cougars are largely night hunters. Furthermore, it is not often such a struggle covers so much ground, for the cougar is one of the most efficient killers among the predators of the world.

In the winter and spring of 1957 I covered almost every square yard of the high grassy slopes above Pass Creek, and counted twenty-eight cougar kills; all but three were mule deer, indicating the sheep are much harder for the big cat to approach and kill.

Certainly there is drama among the peaks the year round where wild sheep roam, drama sometimes painted in blood. But this is the way of nature, all part of a life chain picture relative to wilderness. It can be wonderfully blithe and entertaining, sometimes starkly cruel, but always there is an aura of beauty and an atmosphere of excitement beating like wild drums among the crags and along canyon walls. It is fitting that the most spectacular and beautiful animal should be preyed upon by the continent's most magnificent cat.

3

High Pastures

As boys, my brother and I often rambled the high pastures, green mantles lying across rugged shoulders and flooring basins of the peaks back of our ranch where the bighorns made their home. These were places where creeks tumbled and rushed among the rocks, and waterfalls played in the wind and sun like silver curtains hung from cliffs and ledges. It was wilderness country then without a trail for miles and miles except those made by game and horses. Those of the wild sheep showed in narrow diagonal and lateral lines across the faces of the talus fans, and one could tell how much a trail was used by its width in the loose shale. In places the goats shared these trails, but mostly these white, whiskery climbers could be seen away up on cliffs and chimneys where cool breezes played among remnants of winter snow. Occasionally we would see goats and bighorns feeding on the same slopes; the goats usually above the sheep, for they rarely mingle. Compared to the carefree, lighthearted sheep, goats are dour creatures, phlegmatic and deliberate in their ways unless aroused, and even then no match for the sheep in speed.

In early summer their pastures are the lovely and colorful hanging gardens where hundreds of kinds of alpine flora bloom in brilliant profusion. Nature paints the blooms of the high places in much more brilliant hues than the same ones found at lower altitude. The Indian paintbrush blooms in soft shades of pink at four thousand feet above sea level, but up at eight thousand its flowers are a brilliant scarlet. The same applies to all the rest, for this is a natural compensation to the necessities of pollination, ensuring fertile seed.

At high altitude, the rare dry air rapidly dissipates the volatile perfume of the newly opened blooms, thus taking away the lure which attracts insects that carry pollen from bloom to bloom. So nature in its wonderful way has adjusted by making the blooms there more brilliant, using color instead of perfume to attract insects.

The variety of plants seems endless. One cannot walk in July without crushing blooms at almost every step. At night the mountain wanderer lays out his sleeping bag to slumber in the midst of magnificent gardens listening to the tinkle and murmur of natural fountains. It is a paradise where the wild sheep play and feed belly deep and sometimes over their backs in blooms. When the bear grass spreads its creamy flower heads like great candles three feet high, they appear to be walking corridors all lit with tapers in some kind of pagan ritual of gods, exotic and spectacular.

I have wandered the high plateaus and ridges of the limestone ranges far north in summer and it is the same there, although the floral growth differs some according to the latitude. Most of the northern plants are squat, clinging low to the face of the land; a mingling of dwarf willow, birch never attaining a height of more than two or three inches with various other perennials, and annuals, that make up the rich carpet of the northern tundra. Indeed, it is like treading a vast carpet of varying depths from five to twelve inches deep at two thousand feet elevation to one and two inches deep farther up towards the eternal snowline. Against the rich green of this growth overhung by ice- and snow-draped peaks, the white Dall sheep stand out in brilliant contrast.

At the same time, southward in the desert sierras, the bighorns feed on much different herbage, picking their way among a wide variety of thorns. There is only lushness after rains, and rains come few and far between.

Here by the eastern slope of the Rockies in Alberta, I have had better opportunity to observe some unique feeding habits among the bighorns.

For years I found twin blazes on timberline trees which my old trail partner Bert Riggall told me were the marks of rams butting or rubbing the bark off with the frontal bosses of their horns. Although he had never actually seen them do it, he believed it was to remove the ticks imbedded in the thin strip of skin between the horns that could be reached in no other way. He thought that any ticks that got missed were immobilized by a thick coating of pitch.

It was a logical explanation and theory, but as theories sometimes go, this one was only partly right. One piece of it that did not fit was the fact that the rams selected only pine and fir for their attention. Never did one find a spruce so marked.

One day in late April I was sitting in a grove of red

fir and pines taking the shade from a hot sun, along with a half dozen rams all bedded and lazily chewing their cuds. The place was like a natural cathedral, highly arched, cool and serene. There was a tiny spring bubbling from a patch of green moss amidst a scattering of exquisite pink ladyslipper orchids. Having enjoyed my lunch and a pipe I was about to pick up my pack and move, when one of the rams got to his feet, stretched luxuriously and then walked over to a tree. Suddenly he bowed his neck and began hammering away at the bark with his horns. Pivoting forward and back, stiff-legged on fixed feet, he beat at the bark shredding it till the white cambium layer was exposed underneath. Then he began scraping up the exuding sap with his lower frontal teeth with obvious relish. The secret of the blazes was revealed.

Like many things of a similar nature, once one begins to understand them, much more comes to light. Not only did I see rams blaze trees again, but it became apparent that they revisited these blazes to get more sap, keeping it up till bare wood was exposed and it dried up.

Parallel with this taste for sap, I have seen rams eat the needles of white pine and fir with obvious relish when the slopes were beginning to green up in spring; a kind of diet many zoologists still think is a signal of starvation. But I disagree, for the sheep involved were in good condition and there was plenty of new ground growth to eat. Maybe the sap is a kind of "medicine" to offset the intestinal looseness brought on by new grass and herbs.

Strangely enough I have not observed one shred of evidence indicating that ewes share this appetite for sap and needles. Maybe it is a kind of tonic needed only by rams to recondition their systems after the rut and the long cold winter.

At this time of year, when the perennials are all beginning to grow and the root systems are full of sap, the wild sheep can be seen digging down through loose shale and dirt for roots. Like bears, they are very fond of these, but are not nearly so well equipped to get them. I have seen ewes and rams paw down to a depth of ten inches for the roots of lupine and hedysarum.

Another question remained unanswered for a long time. Occasionally a skull would be found indicating the loss of nipping teeth years before anything like normal old age as indicated by the annual growth rings of the horns.

Then during a blustery session of March weather with intermittent snowstorms, wind and sunshine, came the chance to unravel this bit of mystery. On several occasions over two or three weeks, I saw bighorns scraping rock lichen off the exposed surface of boulders and rocks where it grows in profusion. This is a highly colored, very specialized kind of vegetation looking like heavy paint splashed on the rock; red, yellow, green, grey and black with various shades between. It is among the slowest-growing vegetation in the entire world, taking as much as a century to spread itself over a square inch. It propagates by spores, like the fungi, and is further unique because it is a natural union between the fungi and algae families, and makes use of the special qualities of both to exist where no other plant can grow. Practically nothing is known of its nutritive qualities, but very likely it is high in protein and various minerals which the sheep require in spring.

Their craving for it apparently reaches a point of addiction in some individuals, for a rather small ewe was seen repeatedly working away, scraping the lichen off rocks with her teeth. One afternoon I got within fifteen feet of her as she lay chewing her cud directly above me on a steep slope. As her lower lip drooped, it was possible to examine her teeth through the binoculars. They were worn off almost even with the gums in the middle although her horns showed only five rings. Obviously her life would be greatly shortened by her craving.

I have heard the plains Indians mixed this lichen with kinnikinnick leaves and shredded willow bark to make a smoking mixture, so perhaps it does have a narcotic effect and may be addictive.

At best the life span of the wild sheep is relatively short, like all ruminants (cud chewers), and reaches an average age of ten to twelve years. The oldest ram I ever saw was a bighorn killed on the headwaters of the Oldman River in 1938. It was sixteen, allowing for one year broomed off the tips of the horns. (The term "brooming" refers to the lengthwise splitting of the horn at the end, with many cracks.) The aging of sheep is relatively simple, for each year is represented by a heavy wrinkle on the horn surface made when growth stops in winter. The horn tips of old bighorn rams are nearly always broomed off by rubbing them against rocks to keep the tips of the tight curling weapons from interfering with their vision. This does not occur so often with the stone sheep of northern British Columbia and even less among the white Dalls, for their horns tend to flare out and do not get in the way of their eyes so much.

Over the years as I have rambled and climbed through the finest wild sheep country of this continent all along the mountain chains from Idaho to the far Arctic, one phase of their feeding habits always intrigues me: the use of certain licks to obtain salt and other minerals. This

craving reaches its apex in spring after the long cold
winter, and in some places the sheep come down off the
mountains way below timberline to obtain these necessary
elements of diet. All the grazers share these licks and one
can sometimes observe several species at a lick together.
Even the crag-loving mountain goats come down into
heavy timber to partake of a lick, and I once saw three
moose and nine goats all crowded into such a place right
on the bottom of Beaver Creek Valley in southeastern
British Columbia. It was typical moose country but about
as far from normal goat habitat as one would ever be
found.

Up on the Trout River a bit west of Muncho Lake in
northeastern British Columbia there are some chalky,
hard clay banks along both sides of the stream for perhaps
a mile. In May and June, the stone sheep come in considerable numbers from the mountains for miles around
to paw and lick along these banks, where they excavate
holes and small caves. This is a dry lick in contrast to another kind where a mineral spring or seep carries the salts
and minerals. I have seen sheep licking there in late April
and this activity usually reaches its climax in June. It is
used to a certain extent all summer and fall until winter
locks it up in snow and ice.

Two hundred odd miles to the south there is another
dry lick at the top of some broken cliffs overlooking a
gorge on the upper Prophet River. A band of females
with lambs were observed using it in early August, 1968
—about the time their craving was wearing off, for there
were no signs of heavy recent usage. Perhaps twenty
miles downstream from this spot there is a big hot spring
with a considerable content of sulphur among other elements. This is one of the biggest game licks in the coun-

try, and is used by moose, caribou and sheep. Sometimes one can see all three species there together, and according to Leo Rutledge, this lick is used all year round. Leo has a lifetime of experience in that area as a trapper and outfitter, and his statements on these matters are based on prolonged observation.

I recall a time when Bert Riggall and I found a lick one fall up on the headwaters of the Highwood River in southwest Alberta. We were guiding a hunting party and had been battling our way across an old burn for days. One evening we camped in a small island of virgin spruce forest missed by the fire that had swept that part of the country almost completely clean several years before. It was a welcome change from camping out among skeletons of trees, bleached white by weather and given to falling over in the most unexpected moments. Every time a breeze played across their weather cracks, they set up a discordant wailing like tortured banshees. One had to be very tired or of a particularly fatalistic frame of mind to get a good night's sleep in such a camp, for if the wailing did not keep you awake, the possibility of a tall dead tree falling on your tent made up for it.

So the island of green spruces looked like heaven. It was a snug camp with lots of feed for the horses, unlimited firewood, and a small creek just back of the tents to supply water. But next morning when I went to get a pailful before breakfast, the creek was running stiff with mud, something of a surprise, for the weather had been cloudless for days.

After breakfast we saddled up and rode upstream to investigate. At the top of a twisted canyon under the face of the Continental Divide we found the reason for the dirty water. Eighteen assorted goats were happily messing around in it as they licked at a clay deposit. We herded the goats back up onto the mountain and the creek cleared up again, but for the rest of our stay in that camp we imagined we could taste goat in about everything it took water to prepare. The creek fluctuated between clear and muddy, for the lick was also being used by elk and sheep. It was like camping down a drainage ditch below a stock-yard.

Among many such licks found and observed over the years, the most unique one is on the face of a mountain in a wild canyon not far from my home here on the edge of Waterton Lakes Park. One spring I was out watching a bighorn lambing ground, when I spotted a nanny goat with a tiny new kid coming down off the face of the mountain at the upper end of the canyon. She was scurrying along as though she was heading someplace with something definite in mind and the fluffy little white kid looking like an animated toy had to trot and gallop to keep up, blatting at its mother here and there where it got left behind. The nanny led the way down over a series of steep shelves towards the top of a waterfall coming out of a big snowdrift and disappearing into another fifty feet below. She jumped the stream just at the lip of the falls to proceed down a narrow ledge to one side, when suddenly she and the kid just disappeared. One moment they were there, white as snow against dark rock, and the next they were gone; a now-you-see-a-goat, now-you-don't sort of thing that made me rub my eyes in disbelief.

Before I had a chance to start to unravel this astonishing development, a procession of ewes and lambs appeared out of nowhere coming up the ravine from the opposite direction. A few yards short of the face where the goats had disappeared, they stopped to stand watching something.

To add to the spate of activity, there came yet another goat along the same route the nanny had used, a young billy traveling in the same businesslike fashion. He too climbed down beside the falls and promptly vanished.

I was now thoroughly confused. When a mountain begins swallowing goats before your eyes, it's enough to make even a teetotaler start wishing for strong brew. For at a range of not more than three hundred yards from a good solid position with my glasses glued to my eyes, three goats had appeared to walk up to a solid wall of rock and vanish into it. It was the most perfect natural optical illusion ever encountered. When I climbed out to one side to the tip of a spur offering a different angle, the illusion melted away, and a cave was revealed that from my original position had been perfectly hidden by the angle of the sun on an oblique rock face.

The three goats were visible in the back of it, all busily licking at the wet rock, while out front the ewes and lambs stood waiting their turn to enter. It was an interesting example of hierarchy among species, for big-horns will not enter that cave when goats are using it.

After watching for a while and trying vainly to get into a position where the camera could be trained on it, I came to the conclusion the only way a picture could be taken would be for the photographer to be somehow suspended from a sky hook of some kind over the canyon, so I gave it up. When I climbed to the cave, I found it to be about ten feet wide, eight feet high at the mouth, and twelve feet deep. Along its floor trickles a tiny seep smelling strongly of sulphur, alkali, urine and manure. What is most amazing is the smoothness of the interior, for it has been licked out of solid rock over thousands of years and generations of sheep and goats.

When the larches turn to gold in the fall throughout

the wild sheep ranges, they are sleek with the fat under their hides. By October their new winter pelage is thick and dark colored throughout most of the bighorn country and the southern portion of the stone sheep ranges. Farther north, where the dwarf willow and birch paint the tundra scarlet and yellow, the white Dalls are magnificent with their snowy coats and contrasting gold and bronze colored horns. Now the grasses and forbs have cured on the stem, rich with nutriment. But while the sun hangs low in the south and the northern days are short, the available range for sheep is much less. The conditions they face are tough at best and sometimes unbelievably cruel, but in spite of this, if nothing tampers with their wintering ground, they survive.

While goats do not range farther north than southern Yukon (except in the latitude of coastal Alaska), their wintering grounds are impossible for sheep. They stick to higher country for the most part braving frigid blasts and existing on feed beyond reach of any other vegetating animal. In the British Columbia and Alberta Rockies I have seen where they have walked out on crusted snowdrifts thirty odd feet deep to feed on the lichen hanging from the limbs of timberline spruce and firs. When one looks up in summer to see white goat wool hanging from the branches it is something to make the observer rub his eyes in disbelief unless he knows something of wintering conditions.

Mountain goats seem to have the ability to semi-hibernate for short periods during very hard weather, for when the wind chill drops way down and a blizzard is blowing, they will tuck their rumps into the lee of some shelter and remain almost motionless for days. Then it is possible to walk right up to them. My friend Russell

Bennett, who was on the first ski expedition from Jasper to Banff along the main range of the Rockies many years ago, recounts that he skied up to goats in such weather and was able to touch them with a ski pole. Their whole metabolism seems to slow down to a point of suspended animation and they are very phlegmatic.

The feeding grounds of sheep and goats present a great contrast between summer and winter throughout their ranges except in the southern desert mountains. And so sheep migrate to a limited degree; the goats to a lesser extent. These choose to winter more often than not in places where the difference between life and death seems to be as finely balanced as a bone lying across the keen edge of a hunting knife.

Unfortunately some of the best bighorn ranges have been decimated by the ridiculous, so-called multiple-use program of management to which politicians cling, trying to wring the last dollar out of a very fragile resource. For instance, sheep and cattle have been allowed the wintering grounds of the bighorns in the East Kootenai district of British Columbia, which was, not too many years ago, one of the finest big game ranges of this continent, a mecca for visiting sportsmen from all over the world. But summer grazing and access roads combined to put weakening pressure on the bighorns to the point where they were attacked by lungworm and Pasturella disease (shipping fever in cattle), and they were almost wiped out. From a healthy herd of about 4400-head they dropped to less than four hundred over a period of one winter. If you ignore the aesthetic considerations and look only at the economic ones, this travesty of management still does not make sense, for each trophy ram harvested by a visiting hunter brings into that Province from

$2500 to $6000. At no time in the history of the stock-breeding industry have range cattle ever come close to those prices, especially in view of the limitations of the range involved—the balance spelling the difference to the bighorns.

How long can we pursue these blind roads leading to inevitable poverty and great risk? How long will it take us to realize that we are all part of the life-chain of the environment in which we live? These are vital questions that can only be answered by the awareness and concern of people in general. One cannot entirely blame industry or politics, for these are basically people. The naturalist and concerned ecologist and environmentalist who looks at the broad horizon of the future, realizes that the solutions to these problems lie with informed and caring people of every walk of life. And unless we all wake to the necessity of recognizing the dangers we face, we will all wake up one day economically, physically and spiritually bankrupt.

For we plunder a lovely land in which there can be no joy in fat bank accounts unless we learn to manage.

4

In the Society of Aristocrats

These are the ballet dancers of the peaks, where the winds lift the snow and desert sand in the song of wild country pouring forth its notes in natural cadence through storm-ravaged trees and giant cactus; the frozen peaks of the north, the sun-blasted sierras of desert country and the mountains in between. These are the specialists, the hot bloods, the wonderfully colorful cragmasters, at home among airy castles. They are blithe-hearted adventurers cool-headed in the face of danger, sometimes aggressive but most often delightfully carefree. Given any kind of luck, they can outrun the wolf and outdodge the eagle. Even when they die it is rarely drab, but often cruel and nearly always dramatic, unless they are attacked by the scourge of disease acquired through contact with the tame ones.

The wild sheep of North America, like nearly all associated species, came across the Aleutian land bridge from Asia sometime during the Pleistocene Age, then followed the great ice-free corridor east through Alaska and the Yukon, then swung south through what is now Alberta. Owing to their mountain habits very few fossil bones have been found marking this migration trail, but evidence would point to two separate surges of movement from two different ranges in Asia. The bighorns apparently came first along with the goats, and movement of the great ice mass behind them may have closed the door on any possibility of their populating any part of the north. Then at a later date during an ebb in the ice conditions, the thinhorn Dalls moved in behind the bighorns to populate the region north of the Peace River.

There are still many questions regarding this influx of sheep from Asia that are hanging unanswered. The very best we can do is some educated guessing.

Probably no other facet of their evolution since that time has had so much influence on changing the ways of wild sheep, or been the cause of more fading of their numbers, than their association with man. While many of the early Indian tribes of the plains and mountains, all the way from the tundra country of the north to the desert regions of what is now the Republic of Mexico, did make use of the wild sheep as a source of meat, horn material for utensils and weapons as well as decorations, it was as usual with the intrusion of the white man that the most drastic changes occurred.

Most of the northern tribes—the Hareskins, Slaveys, Beavers, among others—were sheep hunters, although they depended more on moose and caribou for a source of meat. The Stonies and Kootenais were also sheep hunters along both sides of the Divide. The Plains Indians hunted them among the steep river bluffs. Farther south, such tribes as the Pima and Papago Indians apparently made great use of the wild sheep. They made a sort of religious ritual of piling horns, as a sort of spiritual medicine to trap evil spirits bringing bad weather. At a village called Tusconi Moo, a Spaniard named Mange recorded an estimated one hundred thousand horns in one pile in the year 1697. Prior to the advent of guns, the Indian kill apparently made very little inroad into the sheep population, for they were very numerous and their range was spread much wider. But as usual, when the white man and his guns appeared, most of the sheep were killed off and by 1900 had shrunk to a mere handful by comparison. Hunting was conducted largely for meat at that time, whereas now the modern sheep hunter is more interested in trophies.

The first observations of North American wild sheep were apparently made by Coronado's chronicler, one Pedro de Castenada in 1540. One can visualize the Spanish detachment led by Coronado riding up through Eagle Pass between the Pinaleno and Santa Teresa Mountains, the sun glinting on silver horse jewelry and the polished iron of helmets and breastplates. These were the advance-guard handful of Spaniards—the first white men to penetrate the southwestern desert wilderness.

The advance guard saw a flock of wild sheep, and Castenada wrote: "I saw them and followed them. They were large of body, had abundant long wool, and very thick horns. When they run, they raise their heads, and rest their horns on their backs. They are fleet in rough country, so we could not overtake them and had to let them go." A couple of days later, the soldiers found a horn on the bank of the Gila River. To guide Arellano's men, the horn had been placed in a conspicuous place by Coronado, who had then reached a village called Cibola.

Castenada exaggerated upon writing of this horn: "It was a fathom long and as thick at the base as a man's thigh. From its shape it looked more like the horn of a he-goat than any other animal. It was worth seeing. . . ."

At that time the ranges of the wild sheep in North America were much more extensive than they are now, although, contrary to popular belief, the bighorn was never a prairie dweller in the true sense of the word. It was found as far west as the Dakota country along the Missouri and its tributaries. It lived on the steep bluffs along major rivers running east of the Rockies, but never strayed out on the plains beyond running distance from rough ground. Market hunting by early settlers decimated these herds until the only remaining bighorns were left in the mountains, where the steepness of the terrain offered protection from deadly rifles.

There they still survive and do remarkably well in the face of what has been some incredibly stupid management and wasteful intrusion by industry. The worst of this is the multiplicity of roads till there is scarcely a creek that cannot be driven along its entire length by wheeled vehicles. Twenty years ago the rams stayed at and above timberline in comparatively open shoulders, basins and talus fans; they now go down into heavy timber just as soon as open season declares itself with the usual accompaniment of laboring engines and rifle fire. The rifles are too often used at long range by neophytes with no sense of ethics, wounding and frightening animals far beyond reasonable distance for accurate shooting—the result of an illusory power based on the over-rated technical quality of telescopic sights and magnum calibres.

The big old rams, especially, need no further invitation to take to the cover in heavy timber. To successfully stalk and kill a big ram now requires the luck of winning a sweepstake. There is relatively little skill involved and very little of the long distance spotting and stalking that once made the sport so attractive. Now the hunter must resort to endless sitting and watching, waiting for a ram to show himself, and then the stalk will likely resolve into a foot race with other hunters. The sport has degenerated into a kind of pole-sitting marathon with the consequence that most of the old-time, dyed-in-the-wool bighorn hunters have hung up their rifles for good, or turned to the distant hunting grounds of the north.

Having seen bighorn hunting as it once was, and known the challenges and excitement of pitting one's wits and stamina against mountains, weather and wild rams in a setting matched by few others, I have joined those who no longer hunt them with a rifle. I shot a record ram on the head of Castle River in 1954, a beautiful full curl classic kind of head belonging to an old monarch with only two teeth left in the front of his lower jaw, an animal doomed to slow starvation the following winter. The surroundings for that hunt and stalk were about as perfect as they could get, in the company of another old sheep hunter, Ed Burton, who has since taken his last ride beyond the divide; and the memory is good. Such a hunt could never be matched; because it was the ultimate, anything more of the same kind would be an anticlimax. So, from now to the end of my own trail, my sheep hunting will likely be all confined to cameras.

No longer am I fettered by the opening and closing of seasons, or the confines of bag limits or preserve boundaries. I hunt where I please when I please, limited only by leg muscles and time to spend following the great rams. There is still the joy of feeling the keen morning wind in one's face, tasting the salt of sweat after a long hard climb, and the excitement of coming upon sheep at very close range where they choose to allow it—all before putting the trophies on film and letting the sheep go their wild way. There is a satisfaction in knowing one can come back and "shoot" them again another time in a different setting.

There is no question, more wild sheep have been wiped out by the spoiling of their environment than were ever taken by sportsmen. Back in the years prior to 1935, the bighorn ranges of southwestern Alberta between Banff and Waterton Lakes National Parks were the best in the world. For it was here nearly all the biggest record heads originated; huge rams with horns reaching seventeen inches or even more around their bases and outside curl measurements of forty-five inches or higher. But as has happened more recently in British Columbia, the Alberta Forestry Department allowed grazing rights to tame sheep on the vital wintering grounds of the bighorns. The results were catastrophic, for the bighorns had no resistance to such diseases as scabies, lungworm infestation, and virus pneumonia that were introduced by the woolies. They reacted about the same way as the Indians and Eskimos did to white man's diseases and died by thousands.

In the spring of 1936 I left home at the age of nineteen to work for the dean of mountain guides, Bert Riggall, who was likely the most widely recognized authority of his time on the habits of bighorns. He was not simply a great hunter, but a naturalist and photographer. His photos, taken with a very cumbersome camera by today's standards, can still be ranked high among those taken on black and white film. I was introduced to the art of camera hunting by him, a great experience sometimes fraught with a brand of endurance and climbing techniques completely new to me, though I had grown up and reveled in wild country since I was big enough to travel mountain wilderness.

There was a bright clear day in August when we were out scouting for bighorns up along the mountains on the headwaters of the Oldman River. We rode our horses up Beehive Creek to the foot of the mountain bearing the same name, a predominant peak sitting out at the end of a short spur; it was beehive-shaped and sheer cut on its east face.

We tied our horses on a low ridge top overlooking Soda Creek, and with cameras, lunches and rain jackets stowed in our rucksacks, we began to climb. We traversed some talus fans, then worked our way up onto a ridge buttressing the mountain at its back, and from there it was an easy grade to the top. There sitting among lightning pits, we ate our lunch.

From our perch we could see the distant double peak of Mount Cleveland beside Jackson Peak over a hundred miles to the south in Glacier Park, Montana. To the northwest, far out in British Columbia, the snow- and ice-draped fangs of the Bugaboo Range cleaved the horizon. The great tooth, Mount Assinaboine, lifted its head a bit to the north of these on the western edge of Banff Park. There was no hint of haze in the air, and away to the east over the Livingstone Range, the buff-colored rim of the prairie was flat-edged against the sky. We did not know it then, but this wonderful clarity of atmosphere would become something almost unknown. Wild

sheep were our reason for being here, but it was worth
the climb just to sit in the center of this great circle of
mountain wilderness where the only trails were those
made by game or Indians, and some we had cut for our
packhorses.

Two or three years before, we would have been seeing sheep in every direction on the near slopes, but apart
from half a dozen ewes bedded down on a hogback two
thousand feet below, there were none. For two hours
we glassed the surrounding country picking up the odd
bunch of mule deer and a band of elk, but apart from
these the country seemed empty.

Bert finally murmured something to the effect that
if we could find no sheep we could do something else;
stood up and slipped the straps of his rucksack over his
shoulders. He had a gleam in his eyes when he announced
we would shortcut back down to our horses, and then he
took off straight down the south face of the mountain
over a series of broken cliffs and ledges with me trailing
at his heels.

Up to that time I had been nursing the notion of
being quite a climber, but he proceeded to show me some
free-climbing techniques that nearly stopped me in my
tracks. He knew this mountain like the palm of his hand,
and went leaping and bounding down over some short
rock slides like a runaway ram. The various cliffs slowed
him up, but there were plenty of hand- and footholds, and
even though the limestone was a bit rotten, his chosen
route did not diverge much to either side. He had mastered a kind of rhythmic way of going on such a slope
where he never seemed to put all his weight on one foot
or the other, but was in continual smooth motion.

About a third of the way down, he came to a stop

momentarily on a slightly overhanging ledge about ten feet over another slightly wider one below. It in turn hung out over a sheer face about a hundred feet high with a scree of broken boulders at its foot. It was no kind of place to make a slip. It looked impossible to me without the use of a rope, but Bert had other ideas.

Turning his back, he slid his feet out over the edge, found a couple of good handholds and lowered himself to the full reach of his arms. My breath caught in my throat as he let go, twisting himself so he lit facing out with flexing knees taking up the jar. He just looked up at me and grinned, then walked away along the ledge to the top of a broken chimney to disappear down it with his hobnails clattering.

I was left there with two choices: follow him or find my own way. Somehow the latter held little attraction, for I knew he was testing me; so, making use of the same handholds and trying to imagine it was a game being played on a boulder with soft ground ten feet below, I slid over the edge with my back to the scenery. It was about the hardest thing I ever did to let go, but let go I managed to do, trying to mimic his smooth twisting motion. Surprisingly, it was much easier than I anticipated and my landing was good. Taking a big breath, I suddenly knew the exhilarating feeling of mastery of a mountain.

In a few moments I was at his heels again, confident now, even tired leg muscles forgotten. When Bert looked at me, he said nothing, but his eyes were twinkling and there was an expression of approval on his face. The apprentice was making progress, finding out the quality of his guts and, come a day when other people would be involved in an emergency, could hold up his end. Thus

I attended Bert Riggall's private school of the mountains. He had no use for recklessness, but could draw a fine line between danger and easy passage among these mountains.

There were many salutary experiences shared with him; some of them good and some of them sad.

One Sunday in 1936 shortly after I went to work for him, he took me on a ride up onto a mountain ridge back of the ranch, where he often went to stalk game with his cameras. We were looking for sheep, but did not find any. I climbed out to the tip of a rock spur to look down into some scrubby timber below when I spotted something that roused my curiosity. Sliding down into a little pocket, where I could rest my elbows on my knees, I screwed the focus of my binoculars down fine and sharp. I was looking at the bleached-out skeleton of an old ram with a broken horn still attached to the skull. It was familiar, for only a few days before, Bert had shown me a dramatic close-up photograph of this same ram alive shot on a skyline at a range of a few feet. When I pointed it out, Bert was amazed, for the location of his picture was only a few yards away. We climbed down to examine it closer and photographed the bones and skull where they lay, certainly a unique and unusual opportunity to obtain a life-and-death record within two hundred yards of the same spot, though several years apart.

The ram had likely died of old age, but finding that skeleton proved to be a bad omen. For a few days later we were on a climb up along Pass Creek a few miles south amongst the finest bighorn wintering range in the Canadian Rockies. But we found few sheep and they were ragged, forlorn-looking animals. The place was a scene of death, for there were dead bighorns lying everywhere. In perhaps a mile of folded slope we counted sixteen ram carcasses, every one a magnificent full curl specimen. The whole valley was a complete shambles with hardly a live ram left, for whatever disease had attacked them had almost wiped out all the mature males, and there were only a few ewes and young rams left.

I will never forget the look of shock and grim sadness that settled on Bert's face as we traversed those slopes that day. He said little, but what he did opine was prophetic. He suspected the disease that had run through the bighorns like a prairie fire was something contracted through sharing pasture with tame sheep just outside the park to the north, and he was very concerned about it spreading.

As it turned out, his fears were justified; for when some analysis was done, it was found the bighorns had died of a virus pneumonia aggravated by lungworm, a parasitic condition endemic to domestic sheep and cattle. Furthermore, the disease did spread from one end of the bighorn ranges to the other, cutting the herds to a mere handful as compared to their former numbers.

Consequently, what had been a hunting paradise in our part of the Rockies became something else, and our fall hunts often saw us going empty-handed. The bighorns began to recover, but it was a slow process; and it was to be years before they came back to anything like former numbers.

One incident connected with the results of this scourge is still recalled with some disbelief that it could happen to me, although it had its comical aspects.

Like most young guides new to the game, I was not

entirely cognizant of the true importance of the stalk over the kill, or aware that many hunters of experience use the game as a means of escape from the driving pace of city life, and are so selective that the actual shooting is minimal. I was keen to have my clients collect trophies. A hunter accused me one time of wearing him off to the knees to get him up to a trophy, and then giving him the jitters by shaking like a pointer dog on birds while watching the animal and waiting for him to shoot. To say the least I was keen, and what was lacking in experience was made up in enthusiasm. By the shortcomings of youth, I had not yet learned that it is the camaraderie of campfires, living in the open and the satisfaction of being in wild country, which make hunting the great sport it can be. At that time I had known nothing else but wilderness.

It was a fine frosty October morning, the kind of day when just being alive has the taste of something indescribable, a feeling of keen enjoyment that can be savored in no other kind of surroundings. I was guiding a veteran hunter from Chicago, Arnold Schueren, a tough persistent man with a depth of humor and patience; crusty sometimes, even though kind and considerate. I did not know him very well then, but we ultimately became great friends and enjoyed many happy days in high country.

We rode up onto a ridge at the foot of the Continental Divide this morning, tied our horses in a larch grove and sneaked out to its edge beyond to hunker down in a patch of shintangle for a look. Our position overlooked a big basin heading a tributary of the Oldman River. Forming the back wall of the place was a peak towering up against the clear sky, and across from us the south face of a buttressing ridge; its near slope like a green cape hanging from its shoulders, ermine streaked with new snow lingering from a light fall a few days before. To the east of us, the blue-green ranges rolled for miles and miles to a distant sharply-etched skyline. This was bighorn country, the best of what was left of it in southwestern Alberta.

Our glasses swung slowly in search; carefully combing every gully, shelf and slope from the talus fans below to the jagged rims. As usual many of the things momentarily catching our eyes looked like sheep, but turned out to be rocks or tricks of light and shadow. I had glassed this place many times before, had climbed across it from about every angle, and knew it like the well-studied page of a favorite book. Once I had hung precariously between sky and earth at the end of a long rope, the culmination of a somewhat hair-raising descent to retrieve a goat lodged on a ledge after a fall from an upper slope, where a client had shot it. Another time a friend and I had stalked a grizzly here, and upon jumping the big animal at unexpectedly close range, both of us came down with a colossal case of buck fever, and missed him clean with all of at least eighteen shots! This place had history and memories and now my glassing was flavored with familiarity.

Then something came into the magnified field of my glasses away across the basin. It was a fine ram lying asleep on a small green shelf about a hundred yards above timberline. He was dead to the world with his head turned a bit, one horn resting against the ground as they often do to take the weight of their weapons off the neck muscles. The horns were full in the curl and massive. By the time I had pointed him out to Arnold, the excitement had pushed my blood pressure up a notch or two.

It was a tricky place to make an approach with a big chunk of very rough geography to cross before we could get into range. We sneaked back into cover of the timber, then dropped in a big sweeping circle down into the lower end of the basin, thus avoiding possible back-drafts under the peak. Then up through patches of alder and blow-downs we toiled, watching the direction of the breeze by keeping track of some scattered mountain avons fluff that was coursing the wind like snowflakes.

We finally came to timberline and eased carefully up behind a big uprooted tree for a look. A bulge of the slope was hiding the ram, but then I spotted the top of a horn curl showing over the grass about a hundred yards out on the slope. The ram had not moved an inch and was still asleep.

I whispered to Arnold instructing him to just walk out and put the ram up, when a magpie flew up and perched on the horn for a second before squawking in alarm and flying away into the timber. The ram was stone dead! We examined it to find the carcass still fresh, for it had apparently come down off the mountain the previous day and bedded down to die in its sleep. As nearly as could be guessed from a crude autopsy, sometime in its younger years it had suffered from lungworm and partially recovered. There were old, cheeselike pockets of pus in its lungs surrounded by scar tissue. Perhaps because of this misfortune, the ram had never fully grown. What looked from a distance like a noble head was really mediocre, for the whole ram was in dwarf proportions.

Arnold looked at me with eyes twinkling and smiled a little. Later when telling about the experience, he remarked that my face was as long as a fiddler's dream, whatever he meant by that. But my gloom was shattered by his roar of laughter, and then I joined in a good guffaw at an elaborate stalk of a ram that couldn't possibly have cared less if we came or went. The joke was on us, even if it was a bit macabre.

To walk up across the high-hanging basins in summer, where the meadows strewn with wildflowers unfold between stringers of timberline trees and breezes play with curtains of spray from tumbling streams, is to learn much of the vast tapestry of life associated with wild sheep. It is my favorite time of year.

There among the boulder fields the tiny pikas scoot among the rocks busily gathering enormous mouthfuls of herbage to be stacked and cured under overhangs of boulders in the sun for feed during the following winter. These fast-moving, industrious little animals have soft pearl-grey coats, bright black eyes, round ears and inquisitive expressions. For a tail they have something close to nonexistent. They look rather like half-grown chinchillas. They communicate by giving a penetrating bleat, *a-a-a-ay - a-a-a-ay*, a familiar sound to the mountain traveler as far north as the Yukon and Alaska. The only real enemy they have is the weasel and, occasionally, the pine martin; and when one of these shows up in a rock slide, every pika climbs atop its look-out boulder, sounding off with clocklike regularity to warn of the intruder. It is not uncommon to see them gathering their hay from almost under the feet of grazing sheep.

Also associating with the pikas, mountain sheep and goats one finds the hoary marmot—the mountain woodchuck. But unlike the pika, this one eats to put on fat in summer, then hibernates for the winter. They reach a weight of twelve pounds on occasion and wear a silver and fawn-colored coat and a bushy tail. Their eyes are every bit as keen as those of the sheep. The home den is usually dug under a big boulder, which they use as a sort of elevated sentry box to keep a look-out for enemies. Their alarm call, a long piercing whistle, can be heard for a mile on a clear day.

Flying among the limber pines and firs at timberline are the handsome nutcrackers, jays dressed in predominant grey with striking white and black markings.

Their raucous calls mingle with the beautiful songs of many species of birds—varied thrush, Townsend's solitaire, white crown sparrows, kinglets, juncos and many others blend their music with the overtones of breezes among the trees.

It matters not what part of life exists here or anywhere else; each living thing depends on something else alive for its existence, forming an intricate pattern of pulsing beauty. If part of it is destroyed, then the picture loses its meaning and continuity.

So it falls to man to use his intelligence and growing understanding of his association with other forms of life to manage and keep the balances in the face of his own intrusions.

5

Hunting Trails–Past and Present

There has always been an atmosphere of romance and adventure attached to hunting wild sheep—a certain aura of fascination with the challenges and beauty of wild mountain country existing ever since Marco Polo reported the magnificent rams of the sheep that bear his name, which he found amid the peaks of the Himalayas on his epic journey to the silk-draped court of Kubla Khan some seven hundred years ago. Marco's description of this fabulous animal with horns up to seventy inches long stirred the curiosity of the most learned men of his time.

Later, during the height of the British reign in India, many military officers journeyed northward into the magnificent ranges of Afghanistan, Nepal, Tibet and the Kashmir to win their spurs as hunters by stalking the great sheep of those regions. Indeed, the British Army encouraged young officers to spend their leaves hunting these animals to toughen them physically and provide a kind of training logistically valuable in the campaigns against the mountain tribesmen.

In North America the Spaniards first recorded observations of the desert bighorns and were obviously fascinated by these proud and spectacularly nimble animals. During the exploration and settlement of the West, the free-trappers, military people, traders and settlers came to discover the delicious qualities of wild mutton—a discernment putting the bighorn high in value to market hunters and resulting in the decimation of wild sheep from the Mexican sierras to the arctic regions of Alaska and Yukon Territory.

Strangely enough frontier historians make small mention of the mountain goat, no doubt because these animals frequent the highest peaks and roughest terrain. Where big game was concerned, the explorers' interests ran to food and skins; and these did not include wearing out footgear pursuing the white, whiskery denizens of the crags. Mountain climbing held little appeal to the average frontiersman, for he was essentially a horseman, and being mostly interested in provisions, did not pursue goats.

Prejudice may have had some bearing on it, for North Americans have never been partial to goat meat, and very few hunters realize even yet that this is not really a goat at all, but much closer to the antelope species. Compared to sheep, goat meat is inferior. But a fat nanny or young billy properly dressed and hung for a while to age is not to be scoffed at if adequately cooked; it is delicious.

Being no slouch with stew pot and frying pan, and having eaten at one time or another a great variety of things thus acquiring means of drawing comparisons, I can honestly attest that goat meat can be very good. Like all game, it is most important to dress it cleanly and hang it in a cool place for at least four or five days. Unlike cow buffalo, cow elk, young moose, deer or sheep (all of which can be eaten and enjoyed when barely cool) goat meat must be aged, and the longer the better.

As for the savage cave men of twenty thousand years ago or the plains Indians of more recent times, perhaps my appetite and appreciation have been whetted by occasionally knowing what it is like to be really hungry.

To illustrate my point, I once sat in front of the fire with Bill Bacon, a well-known professional photographer, and listened to his account of an adventure. At one point in his career he spent most of a year with the Eskimos up around Point Barrow. Come break-up time, he and a group of Eskimos undertook to come south in an open skin boat along the coast of Alaska. But their plans went somewhat askew when an offshore wind sprang up, trapped them in ice and blew them almost to Siberia. Somewhere out on the Bering Sea they fought their way clear and proceeded by guess and by God to find their way back in peasoup fog and pounding rain. There was no shortage of drinking water because they had to bail the accumulation of rain water out of the boat to keep it from sinking, but they had nothing to eat. Then, when they were really feeling the pinch of starvation, a big rock loomed up with its top lost in the cloud cover hundreds of feet overhead. With gleeful chuckles the Eskimos piled out of the boat to begin climbing the cliffs, for above and hidden in the cloud-muck they could hear the mewing of nesting gulls. Faster than one can tell it, gull eggs began their descent into the boat being passed from hand to hand, dropped and caught in caps, until there were plenty to go around. Then everybody, including Bill, filled up on raw eggs.

Anybody who knows anything of gulls can imagine what it would be like to eat gull eggs raw, especially those well on the way to hatching.

"Sounds like pretty rough grub," I remarked, restraining an impulse to shudder.

"Those eggs tasted just wonderful," Bill assured me, "even the ones with birds in 'em. The difference between good grub and bad grub is about four days going without!"

Of course he was right. In spite of the best plans sometimes a wilderness traveler finds himself knowing what it is like to be really starving, and I am no exception.

But goat meat takes no such priming. However, unlike wild sheep meat, which is delightful roasted, fried or any other way you choose to cook it, goat meat is best treated in the stew pot. Just cut in bite-sized pieces, let it simmer for a couple of hours, then mix in everything you have by way of assorted vegetables. Onions are a must, and if you have none, usually wild ones are available in almost every mountain meadow, although it takes less of these, for their flavor is very strong. Add salt and pepper for seasoning and cook for another half hour. It is a dish fit for kings, gods and hungry mountaineers.

But if the goat happens to be an old and venerable billy, it is necessary to age it for a long time and sometimes even then it's not enough. I once tried to cook some of an old billy not aged nearly enough. The more you chewed a piece of that meat, the larger and more indestructible the piece got. You could take it from your mouth and cut it in half and try again with no better results. The law of diminishing returns did not exactly fit here. I have only met two other animals that compared: one was an ancient buck pronghorn antelope and the other a great-granddaddy Columbia ground squirrel. The meat of all three would have made excellent replacement soles for a worn-out pair of climbing boots.

It makes no difference how old a mountain ram is, just so he is fat. The meat is tender and tasty, a gourmet's delight with any kind of decent handling. But if the ram is so old he is in poor condition, the meat is strong and very tough. To kill a big ram merely for meat without thought of saving the trophy is not justified, unless some mighty unusual circumstances demand it.

Strangely enough the famous Chatfield ram, a stone sheep thought by most authorities to be the finest and most beautiful trophy ever taken in North America, was taken by a meat hunter. Chatfield was a British Columbian hunter and had taken a long packtrain trip exploring north from Hudson's Hope up onto the headwaters of the Prophet River. The party was running low on grub and was about to begin the long journey back to the settlement when Chatfield undertook to kill some meat. What started out to be a mundane stroll for a sheep over a bald-topped limestone dome back of camp ended up with an opportunity to stalk and kill a great ram—a mighty ram with horns that measured 50⅛ inches around the curve of one horn and 51⅝ inches around the other. This ram has held top place in the stone sheep records ever since it was killed in 1938. As near as can be told from study of a photograph, this animal was sixteen years old, the equivalent of one hundred years in a man's age. He may or may not have lived through another winter. He fell to a hunter's rifle, clean killed, and has been preserved as a sort of natural wonder to remind people what can happen when nature and a measure of luck contrive. It is fitting and it is good, for even though long dead, this great ram lives on in history.

The primitive Indians of early times on the plains and in the mountains stalked the sheep with bows and arrows. As has been recounted, they were interested in horns, but not as trophies in the true sense of the word. The Sioux and Blackfeet hunted them along the steep bluffs by the bigger rivers east of the Rockies. Plains Indians were superstitious about mountains and did not hunt there nearly as much as they did on the plains. The Blackfeet occasionally crossed the Rockies to raid among the Kootenais and Flatheads for horses. Once a year, here in Canada, they came in close to the high ranges to cut teepee poles from the groves of slim-boled lodgepole pines, but not to hunt.

The Stoneys were mountain Indians whose hunting grounds extended from the North Saskatchewan down to the region of the forty-ninth parallel. Besides being great sheep hunters, they also pursued the mountain goat and soled their climbing moccasins with this animal's thick spongy neck and rump hide. They were good climbers and trailed their quarry clear to the mountaintops. Bert Riggall once picked up an old and weathered trade knife on top of Black Bear Mountain in what is now Waterton Lakes National Park. Maybe it was lost by some unfortunate Stoney woman, who got a hiding from her man for her carelessness.

Ranging up on the high country between the Peace and Liard rivers, the Beavers were also sheep hunters, as were all the interior natives of northern British Columbia, Yukon Territory and Alaska.

The mountain Indians employed some unique methods in their hunting. The Stoneys made organized drives for sheep and other game by sending the older people, women and children along with all the dogs up the valley bottoms creating a great din. This moved the game up over notches and passes along the well-used game trails where the hunters were waiting concealed in scrub or rock blinds. Sheep, elk and deer, fleeing the racket of dogs and people in the lower country, were thus ambushed, and sometimes considerable numbers were taken in this fashion.

It is doubtful if many goats were killed by driving, for these animals usually take to the most precipitous ground when alarmed. Likely most of the goats were killed by the best hunters, the specialists, and these probably hunted alone or in pairs.

The advent of trade guns made hunting much easier for the Indians. The gun and the subsequent extinction of the plains bison by white men put a great deal of added pressure on other species, resulting in a great scarcity over much of the Rockies. The early guides and outfitters operating in the Alberta Rockies found themselves competing with the Stoneys as late as the early 1920s, and finding trophies was anything but easy.

Some of the earliest records of hunting bighorn sheep in the West are to be found in the personal diaries of early explorers such as John Clark of the Lewis and Clark Expedition. He named the Bighorn River when he came to its confluence with the Yellowstone in 1805 because of the abundance of bighorns there. He didn't know it, but there were even more sheep among the Bighorn Mountains a few miles to the south.

Later, John Frémont wrote of bighorns encountered

during his climb of Snow Peak in Colorado, 13,700 feet in elevation, during the month of August, 1842.

Maximilian, Prince of Weid, a visiting European sportsman, reported seeing bighorns along the Missouri River in the Dakota country in 1833. In this same general area on the same expedition, the famous ornithologist and artist John J. Audubon saw many sheep. He experienced difficulty in collecting specimens, for the Dakota breaks are extremely rough, and likely the hunting was being done by poorly armed, inexperienced men; for at that time Audubon was no longer a young man and likely found such stalking beyond his capabilities.

The famed explorer and mountain climber John Muir, later the original organizer of the Sierra Club, tells of finding evidence that the Indians of Nevada also hunted sheep by driving, but in a more organized and developed way than the Stoneys of Canada.

While climbing in that region in 1894 he found rock blinds built to hold one or more Indian hunters on top of every mountain. These were used in much the same fashion as those of the Stoneys, but some of the mountains showed signs where drives were made by large parties. In favorable spots on high ground these Indians built high-walled corrals out of sticks and rock with long diverging wing fences leading into the gates. Long rows of dummy hunters made of stones were made on flanking ridge tops among which live hunters moved to make it look like possible escape routes were alive with Indians. The sheep were driven and thus guided into the wings and thence into the corrals, where they were surrounded and slaughtered.

My old friend, the late Jack Reid, youngest son of the famous frontiersman, Bill Reid, who was scout for General Crook at the Battle of Rosebud Creek in 1874 and later friend and guide of Teddy Roosevelt on some of his western expeditions, told me an interesting story. In 1890 while hunting wolves, he and his brother, Wallace, surprised three bighorn rams at close range in the badlands a few miles east from Medora in North Dakota. They were carrying rifles and sixshooters, but attempted to catch two of the sheep alive with their lariats. But the rams were too fleet to be caught on such a short run over the top of a small mesa, and before a loop could be thrown, all three rams dropped from sight over the rim and escaped. These were *Ovis canadensis auduboni*—some of the last of the bighorns that once abounded in that part of the country.

Eleven years before, Howard Eaton, one of the well-known family that founded the first dude ranch of the United States, had killed two bighorns on Bullion Butte in the same general region. In a note on the incident, he stated that sheep were very scarce.

By 1899, the Audubon bighorns, which ranged the Dakota country and were about the most eastern-ranging wild sheep of the continent, were a thing of the past. By this time nearly all the bighorns ranging along the rivers and secondary mountain ranges east of the Rockies had disappeared.

Meanwhile, two thousand miles north and west up amongst the mountains of the Yukon Territory and Alaska, the white Dall sheep were beginning to feel the pressure of intruding white men. During the summer of 1896 the whims of fate conjured that two white men, Robert Henderson and James Washington Carmack, were to be involved in the discovery of gold on Bonanza Creek.

Carmack was married to a Tagish woman, and because he knew them so well, was endowed with much of the philosophy of the Indians. And strangely enough, when he and Henderson met at a camp along the Yukon River below the mouth of Bonanza Creek, his association with the Indians put them somewhat at odds—a circumstance that was to cost Henderson much more than he could afford to pay for the indulgence of any kind of personal prejudice. Henderson was a man of driving ambition and had little use for the easygoing ways of Indians. Unfortunately, he made no bones about his contempt for them or a white man who lived with them when he first met Carmack, who was camped with a band of Tagish. Upon being invited to work with Carmack, he turned the opportunity down. Not long after, Carmack struck one of the richest placer deposits ever found on Bonanza Creek, and because Henderson had rubbed him the wrong way, did not send so much as a whisper of his find to him. He did not arrive on the scene till all the choicest claims had been staked.

As a result of this strike and another made upriver, the dying years of the century saw over fifty thousand people living in two frontier settlements of Whitehorse and Dawson City—conglomerations of log cabins and tents that sprang up almost overnight.

Of course the demand for supplies was tremendous and these were largely brought by shallow-draft sternwheel steamers up the Yukon from Alaska. The diggings were a long way from Seattle, the supply terminus, with the consequence that prices were high for everything. Food was especially at a premium and meat was in tremendous demand.

This demand was what motivated Pat Burns, a famous Alberta cattleman, to ship one hundred eighty steers in 1898 under charge of Billy Henry via rail to Vancouver and then north by ship to Skagway, Alaska. The cattle were unloaded there to be trailed overland by way of the pass at the head of the Lewis River and down this stream to the Yukon. By October they were four hundred fifty miles inland in the vicinity of the Five Finger Rapids not far from where the Pelly runs into the Yukon from the northeast. Amazingly enough, they had lost only one steer from a poison plant at this point. Knowing winter was close and the river would soon be frozen, Billy Henry and his crew of cowboys butchered the steers and loaded them on two large flat-bottomed scows. Ten days later they tied the scows up to the bank of the river at Dawson City, where the meat was sold for an average of eighty-seven and one-half cents a pound. Even the green hides were sold for fifty cents a pound to be used for dog feed.

There being only one such intrepid type as Billy Henry and the distances and risks being so great, naturally such a shipment of meat did not begin to fill the demand, and just as naturally the demand soaked up every pound of moose, caribou and wild sheep meat that could be found. Billy Henry made one more successful trip to the gold camps with beef which terminated the trailing of steers into the north. By way of interesting note, this remarkable man still lives at High River, Alberta, clearminded though frail at an age of one hundred four years.

Few records remain of prices paid for game meat during the height of the Klondike gold rush, but undoubtedly much was taken in trade from Indian hunters. There is no question that sheep meat came in for much attention by the many prospecting parties that penetrated almost every valley in the Yukon at that time. Likewise in Alaska

Dall sheep were a prime marketable food source during placer mining days.

At the site of an old cabin built by meat hunters on the upper reaches of the East Fork River just under the face of Polychrome Peak, Olaus and Adolph Murie found a pile of forty ram skulls left by the market hunters operating in that area about 1909 just prior to the designation of this region as Mount McKinley National Park. Although Charles Sheldon in his book, *The Wilderness of the Denali*, mentions encountering meat hunters there in the winter of 1907–08, this cabin did not exist then or he would have mentioned it; he was traveling there almost every day the weather allowed and was camped in a cabin a few miles away, on the Toklat River. Some remnants of the sheep hunters' cabin were still visible when I was there in the summers of 1962 and '63, as were a few portions of corner logs of Sheldon's cabin on the Toklat.

Charles Sheldon was undoubtedly the first and most articulate sportsman to visit the vast hunting grounds of the north, and his two books, *The Wilderness of the Upper Yukon* and *The Wilderness of the Denali*, are classics of printed record concerning the collection and study of wild game.

Like Frederick Selous, the famous explorer and ivory hunter of Africa, who accompanied him on his hunting expedition up the MacMillan River to the Selwyn Rockies in the Yukon in 1904, Sheldon was first an avid adventurer and explorer as well as a first-class naturalist and hunter, who closely studied the habits of the animals he pursued. He was an inveterate sheep hunter passionately fond of stalking the golden-horned rams and enjoying primitive outdoor life in the arctic wilderness.

Throughout the summers and autumns of 1904 and 1905 he journeyed by boat, packhorse and on foot into the rugged mountains of country drained by Coal Creek and the MacMillan River, both tributaries of the Yukon.

The following year he made an expedition into the heart of the Alaska Range near the foot of Denali, the highest peak in North America, later incongruously renamed Mount McKinley. Again in 1907 he returned to the same area across country by packtrain in the company of an Alaskan named Karstens. They built the cabin previously mentioned in a grove of black spruce near the Toklat River. Sending the horses back out to suitable wintering ground, he and Karstens spent the winter there with a dog team as means of transportation, collecting wildlife specimens and observing the habits of the Dall sheep.

The more he saw of this magnificent mountain region, the more Charles Sheldon was convinced that it should be set aside as a national park; and upon returning to New York he was largely instrumental in influencing the powers in Washington in the ultimate formation of Mount McKinley National Park. Henry Karstens, a very remarkable man in his own right, was subsequently made the first superintendent of the park, and made the first ascent of Mount McKinley by way of the route now known as Karstens' Ridge.

From the time I learned to read, every scrap of literature dealing with northern British Columbia, the Yukon and Alaska has been devoured. When Charles Sheldon's books fell into my hands they were read and reread with utter fascination sparking a determination to someday see the country he so vividly described. But even with my built-in curiosity to see what was over the next ridge and my fascination with wildlife prodding me, it was many years before the opportunity arrived.

In 1959 the chance came, fifty-odd years after Sheldon wintered in the wilderness of the Denali. That year I was offered the opportunity to help organize an expedition into the western Yukon in the mountains adjacent to Kluane Lake to capture alive some Dall sheep lambs and a ewe. The lambs were to be kept at the Alberta Game Farm near Edmonton, a zoological park founded by the well-known Al Oeming. The ewe was to be consigned to the Canadian Government Experimental Station at Haines Junction, Yukon Territory. This expedition was my introduction to the northern wilderness with its fabulous richness of wildlife; it led to other expeditions, which gave me the opportunity to personally retrace some of Charles Sheldon's old trails as well as many new ones.

Many times I have stood on a ridge top overlooking miles and miles of arctic mountains, where the peaks stood up clear to the far horizon, rank on rank for a hundred miles or more against the clear blue of the sky. I have looked down on the mighty Yukon sweeping down between the hills like molten silver in the sun, a giant water road used by the hordes of prospectors during the golden era of placer mining seventy-odd years ago. One could imagine what it looked like then, with small boats and paddle wheel steamers plying its length. My trails have led me through the towering peaks of central Alaska around the foot of Mount McKinley across the rich green carpets of tundra stretching in undulating pitches and folds across the valleys from snowline to snowline.

One time we flew down the great canyon squeezing the Mackenzie River between the mountain ranges of the

Northwest Territories, riding a Grumman Goose under a thick overcast. Below us the surly yellow river rolled, eddying and boiling from the pressure of ungiving rock. Above us the mountain ramparts were hidden in soupy fog and rain. Unaccountably the bearings of the generators of each of the motors had burned out within five minutes of one another, an unheard-of coincidence, for the twin motors were in no way dependent on each other and ran on completely separate systems of fuel and ignition. Pilot Warren Instrom was trying to beat a weather front to Inuvik and the services of an engineer, when we flew around a bend of the river to be confronted by a solid wall of storm and rain. Putting the plane in a tight turn, he doubled back between the walls of the canyon and I imagined a slight scraping noise as we banked past rock on either side. We landed the amphibian on the gravel strip at Norman Wells in a nasty crosswind and stayed there until repairs were made.

The interval gave us an opportunity to look at this magnificent valley carved between mountain ranges, a place that was once part of a great ice-free corridor, a refugium that existed during the Ice Ages. It was the route by which most of our North American big game species and all the native tribes found their way from Asia into this continent with the exception of the Incas and the Aztecs. To the west, the Mackenzie Mountains are the home of Dall sheep, but to the north and east there are none even though some of the country is almost identical, for at one time this portion was likely a mile deep in ice. Later the river formed an effective barrier to the wild sheep, for they are not habitual swimmers like moose and caribou, and they do not migrate in winter. There are mountains east of the Mackenzie where Dall sheep would do well, but so far no introduction has been attempted.

Another time I took a four-wheel-drive truck carrying a camp outfit over the pass from the headwaters of the Klondike River along the famed Demster Trail. It was in the country to the eastern end of the trail towards Fort McPherson where Demster and his party perished from cold and hunger half a century ago.

It was mid-August when a friend, Earl Ward, and I dropped down the far side of the pass across the great rolling flats along the upper reaches of the Blackstone River. On either side of the valley the ranks of limestone domes rose sharp cut against the blue of a clean-washed sky. This is caribou and sheep country, but the caribou feed there only in winter, and apart from some distant white spots on a ridge top, we saw no sheep. The trail was a sketchy one made some time before by prospectors with a bulldozer. Sometimes we had to quit it, where washouts cut it off, and take to the river bed. We camped lower down on the Blackstone in the first green timber, where we could see east through the Ogilvie Mountains. We set up the tent that evening at least one hundred twenty miles from the nearest occupied dwelling, and while we were busy with various chores, a giant grey timber wolf came out of the willows about a hundred feet away to inspect our camp. We must have looked too hard and directly at him, for he became self-conscious and disappeared as quickly as he came. The wolf, some ptarmigan, a host of ground squirrels, and some arctic grayling we caught, were the only wildlife we saw in that vast stretch of country—apart from the distant sheep. As usual when one travels by truck unprepared to move and camp away from it, there is little game to be seen.

In the summer of 1962, my two oldest sons and I took

a boat to Mush Lake west of the Haines Highway. From there we went down the lake to its outlet, portaged around a falls at the top of the Bates River, and thence down the Bates Lake to a campsite on the river again.

This is one of the most beautiful mountain and lake regions in all the north, a paradise of sparkling blue water framed by ancient spruce and snow peaks like great fangs. Unlike most of the Yukon, it is deep snow country in winter inhabited by moose, grizzlies, black bears, goats and a few wandering caribou. There are no sheep there, but we counted twenty-seven goats in one bunch up on the top end of Iron Creek, proof again that these animals can live where no sheep can exist. This is very close to the northern limit in latitude of the North American mountain goat range. A few miles to the north where the snow lies shallow in winter and the wind whips the ridges bare there are plenty of sheep where the Dezadeash River cuts west through the Alseck Mountains to join the Alseck River a hundred miles or so east of the Yukon-Alaska border.

It is all part of the great eleven thousand square mile Kluane Game Preserve, a region now set aside as a national park by the Government of Canada. No part of what is left of the wildernesses of the world better deserves the distinction, and it is to be hoped that the Canadian people overcome their love affair with resource exploitation and desecration and their feeling of false security in the growth-and-development syndrome in time to see the enormous value of preserving this area as it now stands. It forms a truly living museum of the mountain, lake and tundra country of Canada's north.

Almost every year for seven years I traveled by plane, horses, packdogs, automobile, boat and on foot through the vast reaches of mountains and valleys between the Mackenzie River and the central ranges of Alaska. I have looked off the starboard wing of a plane at the yellowish waters of the Beaufort Sea where the Mackenzie spills its silt, and then away to port where the ragged crests of the Richardson Mountains lift against the horizon. These are sheep mountains, home of the snowy Dalls.

Given half a dollar for every mile we walked through such country, my sons and I would be very rich men. The skin on top of our shoulders grew thick from the pressure and rubbing of packboard straps. We know what it is to be lean and hungry. We have also savored the satisfaction of being in top physical condition, almost as hard and tough as the sheep and wolves sharing the mountains with us. We rambled carefree with the golden-horned white sheep, knowing the happiness and serenity of mind that goes with being alive in that vast arctic land.

More than once it was possible to stand in almost the exact spot described by Charles Sheldon so graphically, and look at sheep where he saw them. It was something of a satisfaction, a cheering thing, to note that there were many more sheep than when he saw that country half a century before. The protection of law, the formation of preserves and the ceasing of market hunting have had their favorable effects.

Too bad the bighorns have not been so lucky. From the Peace River to Mexico, outside the restrictions of national parks, the wild sheep country has been torn wide open, the environment scarred and broken by the false political altruism labeled as multiple use. It is in fact the giveaway of rich natural resources and the legalized takeover of publicly owned lands by private interests. It is anything but multiple use, for some of the finest recreation grounds and waters have been utterly wasted. There is no way by which much of this loss can be justified on a long-term basis; but what hurts the most is knowing that by taking a little more time and exacting a bit more planning, most of the benefits of such things as coal, oil and timber could be utilized without the waste.

It is again proof that we have progressed fast and far in our development of technology, much faster and farther than in our accumulation of wisdom. We have succumbed to the blandishments of quick profit, the demands of luxury living and the energy hunger of the industries supplying it without thought of the limits of resources that this spacecraft known as Earth can supply. We have made a religion of technocracy without much regard of the future of the people using it. We accumulate wealth —most of the time much more than we need in material —with no comprehensive admission that as ingenious as scientists and engineers can be, nobody has as yet figured out how to build pockets in coffins.

If we must do everything with economic values in mind, we are strangely blind; for we continue to overlook such things as the value of wildlife. A trophy bighorn ram grosses the province or state where it is taken by a visiting hunter an average of three thousand dollars or more, and the same applies to other kinds of game. How can we countenance the loss when wasted environment cancels such assets? How do we balance the books over the long haul where futures are considered?

When I first rambled the country between Banff and Waterton Lakes National Parks, this stretch of the Rockies was by virtue of its beauty and resources among the finest recreational areas of the world. Here the bighorns attained the most massive horn growth, apart from the fishing which was marvelous. The top bighorn trophies were taken from this region.

It was here on the head of Oyster Creek in 1924 that Martin K. Bovey collected a trophy ram that held first place in the Boone and Crockett records for many years. He was a young man then hunting with Bert Riggall, and the hunt was a classic one—not really difficult, but a kind of planned stalk dealing with a specific animal. The atmosphere that historic morning was stiff with excitement and anticipation as he and Bert crawled through a boulder field. When the range closed to something like two hundred yards, Martin choked back an impulse to come apart from sheer nervous pressure, and made a clean killing shot. If he lives to be a hundred years old, he will never forget the indescribable thrill of stalking that great ram amongst a wilderness of snow-capped shining mountains, where the clouds overhead were running against the blue on a soft southwest wind. The hunters, because they truly loved the country and the game they hunted, were not alien to the picture; they were part of it and following an urge ages old. Martin was wise enough to know that anything else by way of a sheep hunt would forever be nothing more than an anticlimax and he never killed another sheep. Instead he turned to cameras and became a successful professional wildlife photographer.

While this hunt was taking place, there was another bighorn trophy hanging on the wall of a homestead cabin owned by a rancher named Fred Wyler not three miles from Bert Riggall's headquarters, just north of Waterton Park—the same place we still occupy.

Fred Wyler was not really a hunter, but one fall day in 1911 he decided to go out after a bighorn sheep.

Several of his neighbors had killed bighorns in the vicinity. One man, Henry Mitchell, had stalked and killed a big old ram with fine horns that Fred admired. So he sallied forth with his .30-30 Winchester on horseback up a short tributary of Yarrow Creek about an hour's ride from his door.

Being new to the game, it can be supposed he was pretty casual about it and not overly concerned if he got a sheep or not. But in a very short time, he spotted a big lone ram, and it happened to be in a place where stalking was not much of a problem. Fred slowly made his way within range, rested his rifle over a convenient boulder and dropped the ram dead in its tracks.

The ram was very old with an extremely massive pair of horns—big and impressive enough that Fred recogniz it as something special and had it mounted by the local taxidermist. This bighorn trophy hung on his wall until he died, when it was inherited by his nephew, Clarence Baird.

Clarence valued it more as a keepsake than a trophy. Several times over the years, acquaintances and neighbors suggested he have it measured by an official scorer of the Boone and Crockett Club, but he just shrugged the idea off. Then an official scorer heard about it and came with his steel tape to measure it. After carefully tallying the score, he rubbed his eyes in disbelief and measured it all over again. Over fifty years after it had been killed, it thus became officially the largest bighorn ever taken in North America.

But quite recently, on December 11, 1971, this huge old bighorn trophy was completely destroyed in a fire that burned the Baird ranch house to the ground.

As I write this, two beautifully mounted bighorn ram

trophies look down off my wall. The largest was taken by my father-in-law, Bert Riggall, with whom I shared many a trail in the Rockies and a thousand campfires. It was taken within four miles of my door near the extreme source of Cottonwood Creek in the late autumn of 1906 about four years prior to that region being surveyed to become a part of Waterton Lakes National Park. It stands high in the record book, but it is not altogether this fact that makes it valuable to me. It is a reminder of great days shared with a remarkable man among the mountains; it evokes memories of a wonderful personality I was fortunate to call friend, and it all adds up to a part of local history to be recalled with nostalgia but will never be the same again.

The other is the ram I stalked and killed while hunting on the head of Castle River a dozen miles farther west in the fall of 1954. This, as I said earlier, will likely be the last bighorn I will ever kill. Sometimes good memories are more likely to stay that way if one does not strive too hard to emulate them.

6

High Country Honeymoon

People, whether they realize it or not, have always been influenced by other forms of life associated directly or indirectly with them in their environment. Primitive man always was and still is, in various parts of the world, a hunter depending on his success with many kinds of weapons ranging from fish hooks to bows and arrows for means of life.

Contrary to the conviction entertained by those who tend to support complete preservation, classing the hunter as a blood-hungry barbarian, a throwback from so-called civilization to the savage, the true sportsman hunter, really loving the game, is an asset to wildlife of all kinds. It is these who dip deep into their private bank accounts to support the causes of organized conservation and without them such organizations that are dedicated to wetlands restoration, many forms of research and other valuable projects would be nonexistent.

To practice complete preservation in any society is

the next thing to impossible, and furthermore contrary to nature. People who advocate it are not really very consistent and tend to overlook a valuable facet of outdoor recreation, plus the fact that we are not really so far along the trail from the primitive that we have lost the built-in characteristic of wanting and needing to hunt.

Among the wide variety of people, of many walks of life, finding their way every year to my door from all corners of the world, there are some who abhor hunting, will not eat meat and subsist on vegetation because they sincerely feel this is best for them—anything else assaults their aesthetic souls. This is fine and I cheer them for it. It is the privilege of any individual, but as in the case of expounding one's particular brand of religion, I personally feel rather strongly against such a belief being thrust down someone else's throat.

Besides, while a few purists go as far as to wear canvas and rubber footgear and a string for a belt, there are others sufficiently hypocritical to wear leather footgear and hold up their pants with a strip of the same material. These are the noisiest of the lot, and on more than one occasion have had a turn at me.

I have often tried to analyze my own approach to hunting in such a way that it could be explained to others who might justifiably question the ethics of a conservationist who enjoys such recreation. It is not an easy thing to do, because I truly love to be around animals ranging free and undisturbed and certainly do not look on wildlife as just something put there for my enjoyment or to be killed. Perhaps it can best be defined thus: conservation in its truest form is a situation where man and nature work in harmony together. Hunting, properly managed and conducted with decent ethics, is most definitely a part of that harmony; for it is of no detriment to any species to take a part of each year's crop, a portion of the natural increase, to keep it within bounds of the restrictions of wintering range. It is equally necessary to maintain a very important phase of recreation. Man is inherently a predator, whether or not he chooses to recognize the fact, and because he is somewhat predatory he needs this outlet. It is the establishment of good ethics that counts. Under such discipline and awareness, he can be a powerful and successful influence towards the preservation of environment and the continuance of the wildlife he pursues.

Why do I hunt the wild things I love? In fact my guns are hung up and now used largely for putting holes in targets, but I still enjoy singling out a buck in the fall and taking him to add to the winter's food supply. It does something for my ego as a provider for my family —a certain pride in the heart of man since he first picked up a stone to throw it and bring down a bird or animal for food way back there when a fire stick was the means to make a fire to cook it. Besides we are very fond of fat, prime venison. Although we don't think of it in that way, it can be classed as rent paid by one animal for the food and shelter many others of his kind enjoy inside our fences. Also I have many friends who are hunters, and they are the salt of the earth. I still very much enjoy taking the trail with them in big open country and sharing a fire and the contents of a frying pan, stew pot and the brew from a tea pail.

There are few families alive who have benefited more from their association with wildlife and the kind of people who love to hunt than those who share my roof. The advantages we enjoy go infinitely deeper than mere money gained from our activities afield; no question, they began when we were still in the cradle. But it was not till we were old and experienced enough to observe the richness of our surroundings that we became aware of them, and by one means or another began answering the calls of destiny.

Thirty-two years ago this last June, I helped trail a string of forty-five horses north from this ranch to our base camp on Dutch Creek near where the Oldman River twists its way east through the Gap in the Livingstone Range out onto the rolling reaches of the Alberta prairie. The hills and valleys along the front of the Rockies were lush and green, the sun warm and the breeze redolent with the smell of flowers and new leaves on the aspens and willows. On the ridge tops between the many streams across our path, one could sit his saddle and see the mountains stretching from south to north—blue and mauve in the distance. The sound of the Swiss bells on the horses played music in accompaniment to the sound of hoofs; muted on the grass, then drumming on hard trails. The timing of the bells chimed slowly when we walked up the steep slopes and over rough ground, but picked up its rhythm when the horse herd broke into a long reaching trot on the flats.

At first the horses were spooky and fractious after the winter's complete freedom, but after two long days on the trail both men and animals were once more a well-organized unit, blending together with the smell of hot dust and sweat in their noses. There was a certain anticipation of mountain trails ahead stretching through summer and fall till snow and cold sent us back to the home ranch for the winter.

I knew a feeling—a satisfying awareness that my

personal trail held promise, although it did not stem from accumulation of much property. For about all I owned in the world besides what I stood up in was my saddle and bedroll, the contents of my war bag, a few horses, traps and various gear. This was the beginning of my third year as a guide, packer and rough string rider, and experience was telling me something of the zest going with being fairly good at what I was doing. For three years I had been attending a kind of outdoor school under the direction of Bert Riggall, a man who was a great teacher without being aware of it. The horses had added their bit to the education, as well as the association with many highly educated people. The school of the Rockies is one of hard knocks on occasion, but it has its definite compensations.

When we came jingling into the corral at Dutch Creek on the evening of the second day with ninety miles unrolled behind us, camp was set up and waiting. Bert greeted us as we pushed the horses through the gate. After unsaddling, I left my trail partner to tie up a night horse and headed for the cook tent suddenly aware that I was starving. At the door of the tent I was happily greeted by the girl who reigned over the place. I had not seen her for two days and it seemed like two years, which speaks for itself.

Bert's daughter, Kay, had been born in a tent and grew up on horseback. She had worked on the trail as cook for the outfit since she was fourteen years old and had an uncommon amount of experience for her years in about everything from keeping city people happy in wild country, to treating an axecut in somebody's foot, or making a sick horse well again. Her smile was serene and her temper about as even as a woman's can be. Many times, I have seen her get off her horse in pouring rain, help set the cook tent up and have a sizzling hot supper ready for a dozen people in about forty-five minutes from time of arrival.

Kay and I had been working on the same crew for two years, so we knew each other. There is no place where you get to know anyone quite as well as while camping in all kinds of weather on wilderness trails, especially in the fall high up in bighorn country. For there the blinds are lifted, the true character of a person is revealed, and there is no man or woman who can manage to hide much of importance about themselves. There is something about living in the open among high mountains in all kinds of weather under canvas with the smell of campfire smoke in your nose that strips away all pretense.

To make a long story of fun and adventure shorter, after four solid months on the trail with various parties that summer and fall, Kay and I were married on a fine October day at high noon in front of the big windows of the lodge here at the ranch and headed out on our honeymoon. Did we take off for the city and the bright lights? We did not. We saddled up nine head of hand-picked horses and headed back into the mountains for a month's sheep hunt. We did not care a whoop if we shot a ram, but we knew the quest would take us a long way, we would have a wonderful time with nobody to think about but ourselves. The hunting was strictly an excuse for the going, but if we were lucky we would come back with the winter's meat.

We traveled in leisurely fashion following the streams up between the mountains under brilliant skies with the lower slopes all painted in yellow, gold and red. We pitched our tent on mountain meadows in the evenings close to a stream, and while I tended the horses, Kay cooked supper. We ate from a folding table sitting on pack boxes with our aluminum plates gleaming in the light of candles, and what was just plain good food tasted like a feast prepared for gods. We lay snug in our eider-down robes at night drifting into sleep with the soft murmuring of the river in our ears accompanied some-times by the music of Swiss bells in the distance, or the faraway lonesome singing of coyotes.

Sometimes we took our fly rods and went fishing with the barbs of our hooks broken off to make releasing the trout easy. At one camp we checked the sights of our rifles by shooting at a white spot on a boulder projecting from a bank two hundred fifty yards away across a bend of the river.

It was just after sunrise and Kay was getting ready to shoot from a prone position behind a rolled-up sleeping bag, when we spotted two riders coming up the valley. They were cowboys from a big ranch outside the moun-tains making their fall round-up of the cattle grazing here all summer. We knew them and after the usual greetings, they asked what we were shooting at. When I pointed to the target, they both looked at Kay, and one said, "Hmmm," softly to himself and there was a slight note of skepticism in it. I just nodded and grinned at her as a signal to go ahead and shoot, while our visitors stepped off their horses to watch.

Kay rested her left hand holding the forestock of the little .250 Savage over the sleeping bag, snuggled her cheek down firmly on the stock, and squeezed off a shot. Dust flew from the mark on the rock. She levered a fresh round into the barrel and fired again. Again the

bullet kicked up dust from the same spot. Casually she
stood up to let me take my turn. The cowboys were looking at her with awe and admiration, for there are few
things that impress this kind more than good shooting.

As they stepped up on their horses, the skeptical one
swept off his hat in a graceful bow from his saddle and
said, "Some shooting ma'am! Good hunting!" Then turning to me he added, "Congratulations! But take care you
don't ever make her mad enough to take a shot at you,
because if she does, she sure as hell ain't going to miss!"

With that they whirled their horses and were gone.

There came a day when we rode high above timberline along the crest of a ridge, glassing a series of basins
for bighorns. But all we could find was a bunch of
ewes and lambs and a few juvenile rams. We watched
them a while from above, our saddle horses ground-
hitched behind us over the rim out of sight, but there
were no big rams in the vicinity. A mile or two of country
was covered like this, and then we ate lunch on top of a
rocky point while glassing the surrounding country.
About a mile away, I spotted a big mule deer buck with
a fine rack of antlers as he got up out of his bed in a
patch of shintangle to feed along a strip of low brush
at the foot of a rock slide. We needed meat and here was
a chance to get it, but the buck was in a very open piece
of country with very little cover for a stalk. While we
finished our sandwiches we looked the problem over and
decided the only way to reach the buck was to come down
from above him on the far side.

So leaving our horses we made a great circle way
up around the head of the canyon. Our swing took us
more than an hour and finally brought us to a place
directly opposite where we had first spotted the buck.

The only wind was from the thermals lifting up the slope in our faces in the warm sun. Making use of the folds of the slope we headed down. Then we came to the long stretch of coarse rock slide above the patch of scrub where the buck had been feeding. A slight bulge just over the spot hid it from us, but our hobnailed boots would telegraph our approach long before we could come within range.

There was just one thing to do: sitting down I took off my boots and hung them over my shoulder. Not hesitating a moment Kay did the same and together we went gingerly out onto the broken stuff in our stocking feet. One thing about going over rough rock with nothing on your feet but a pair of heavy wool socks, you are inspired to proceed with care and are consequently very quiet about it. So we went down across the slide as silently as a couple of Indians.

Finally we came out onto a tiny grassy spot within sight of the scrub willow, but no buck was in sight. Combing the place with the glasses, I examined every little detail of it with great care. The lenses picked up the dull gleam of a polished antler point sticking up from behind a boulder a hundred yards below.

Whispering to Kay to get ready, I threw a rock down the slope. The buck must have been aware he had company, for he soared out of his bed in a great leap and went bounding down the mountain. After half a dozen jumps, he paused to look back and there Kay dropped him with a quick shot through the heart.

The echoes of her shot had not died, when another, much bigger buck exploded out of some shintangle not twenty yards to my right. He took me completely by surprise and by the time I got swiveled around, was flying in great jumps down the mountain. Swinging the little 7 mm Greener-Mauser like a shotgun, I swept the sight past his nose and closed my hand on the trigger. The bullet caught him in the ribs on top of a great bound, raking through at a forward angle and dropping him so dead he never kicked.

Both bucks were hog-fat. There was something mighty satisfying about cleaning them out and cutting up the carcasses so they could be packed on horses; the days were growing shorter and the nights sharp with frost, reminding us of the long cold months ahead when fat venison would taste mighty good. I hung the quarters in a scrub pine to cool.

As we were closer to camp than to the saddle horses, I suggested to Kay that she walk down the canyon to the tent pitched at its juncture with Savanah Creek, while I made the long climb back up to the horses and brought them back around the way we had come. To this she readily agreed and she disappeared down valley with her rifle slung over her shoulder. Little did I think that the day's excitement was far from being over.

Some time later when the sun was just beginning to dip behind the mountains to the west, I was skirting the face of a steep grassy slope along a narrow game trail with Kay's horse trailing behind. I was still more than a mile from camp, relaxed in the saddle with my mind on the hot supper that was waiting ahead, when the game trail lifted a bit to skirt the top of a low bank rimming a hole full of brush. There was a spring bubbling up among the willows with a big lone spruce growing beside it. My horse was a big, black, quarter-bred Kentucky mare, and when she got right above the spring hole, there was a sudden great snort from something hidden in the brush below and another from the mare in reply. Then a big grizzly reared up, and the horse promptly blew up. Being very allergic to bears, she swung her nose uphill and reared straight up on her hind legs. Swiveling in the saddle and drawing my rifle in the same motion, I was looking down over the cantle squarely into the grizzly's face. The mare was apparently going to try to kill the bear by falling on him, and wanting no part of such recklessness I swung off her. At the same time she gave a great jump and I came down from a great deal farther up than I planned with my rifle clutched in my hand. The landing shook me plenty and slowed me down, and by the time my eyes came back in focus and I got somewhat better organized, the bear was just disappearing over a bulge on the slope below heading for tall timber in great bounds. When I looked back towards the horses, it was to see them hightailing for camp on the dead run.

Somewhat chagrined and disgusted, I followed. About a quarter of a mile from camp, Kay came riding to meet me leading my horse. When she saw I was still in one piece and not even limping, her face lit up and when I explained what had happened she laughed.

"Hurry up, bear hunter!" she said. "Supper will be burned to a crisp."

Whirling her mount she headed back on the gallop. Lifting my horse into a run behind her, I couldn't resist howling a warwhoop of sheer exuberance. It was fun to be alive. This was adventure raw and wild; we were up to our ears in the middle of it.

At supper Kay told me how she had come down through timber along the creek; big branchy white pines loaded with cones, and the ground beneath all torn up by grizzlies digging up squirrel caches. That year the white pines in that part of the country bore a heavy crop of nuts, and as they always do, the squirrels had gathered from miles around to reap the harvest. The same moccasin telegraph had told the grizzlies and they too came, not to take the nuts from the cones in the trees, but to rob the squirrel caches. Kay reported the ground was literally plowed under the trees and that she had come a mile ready for trouble, parting the greenery ahead of her with the muzzle of her cocked rifle.

Next day when we went back with horses for the meat, we crossed the tracks of four grizzlies, but none had touched our meat.

Grizzlies did not interest us enough to go out of our way hunting them, so again we packed to head up onto the slopes of the main range of the Rockies just a mile or two east of the Continental Divide.

It was a wild and secluded place we chose for a campsite, our tent snuggled in close to a grove of big pines on a bend of a little creek with snow-streaked peaks towering up behind. It was a dream kind of hunting camp with shelter, water, lots of dry firewood for the cutting, and plenty of good grass for the horses along a chain of meadows flanking the meandering stream. Apart from an old Indian trail marked with blazes made with knives, round-backed instead of flat like those slashed by a white man's axe, the valley looked like nobody had visited it for years. Except for the hooting of a great horned owl in the trees back of the tent, it was very quiet that evening as we ate supper by candlelight.

Next morning it was blowing hard, but it was warm so we went out to have a look for sheep. A couple of miles to the west, the trail lifted steeply out of the timber into a series of alpine meadows just under the talus fans of a big basin. The wind was sporadic but very turbulent, alternating between periods of flat calm and wild gusts that came roaring and twisting through the timberline spruces and larches. Overhead, the sky was full of flying, wind-torn clouds scudding eastward on the blast of a southwest gale. Up high the wind was consistent in its direction but down at our level it was sucking back under the cliffs, very erratic and promising trouble if we had to make a stalk.

Sheep trails crisscrossed the slides, some heavy and looking freshly used, but when we tied the horses and climbed up for a closer look, the freshest sheep sign we found was two or three days old. In this kind of weather tracks age fast, which can be misleading, but when we glassed the slopes no sheep were in sight. We climbed down to remount and head up onto a ridge dividing this basin from the next one to the south.

Tying the horses again in a little grove of scrub fir lining a pocket, we climbed to the crest and there ran into the full blast of the wind. Crawling on hands and knees we bellied down to glass the deep basin revealed below. The wind was terrific, stinging our faces with bits of herbage and dirt, sometimes forcing us to flatten out with eyes tight shut for protection. Overhead it was booming and slatting off the top of the cliffs as though popping giant sails.

Directly across from us at a fairly high level where a strip of slide rock lay trapped between cliffs, there were a couple of snow-filled gullies showing the tracks of sheep. These tracks looked fresh, so we endured the discomfort and continued to search in the intervals allowed by the wind. We would not dare try any kind of stalk across the ledges along the front of the mountain on a day like this, for it would be far too dangerous. But the rams would likely be low in this kind of weather, if they were here at all, and that was where we directed our glasses.

We were about to give up, when I saw a flicker of movement in a strip of brush away across the basin, low near the timber in the bottom. Then the outline of a big pair of curling horns showed up against a patch of yellow leaves, and a moment later six rams filed out of the willows to begin feeding on a strip of grass. Two were young with half-curl heads. Three more carried horns close to a full curl. The leader was a magnificent old ram —the kind that makes the pulse of a hunter jump. If they had been warned of our coming they could not have chosen their feeding ground with a better eye to strategic location. It looked like an impossible place to approach, particularly on a day like this with the wind rolling and curling back under the lee of the mountain in all directions. It was not only being stirred by the sheer force of velocity, but it was warm and this compounded thermals into the boiling cauldron brewing a hunter's nightmare, and my experience knew no precedents from which to draw comparisons. There were two things that were sure: these rams would be gone if they caught our scent and if they saw us they would be rapidly departing through a hole in the scenery. My memory was fresh with an example of their keen eyes.

Earlier that fall, Bert and I had been hunting in this same general region with our old friend Franklin Crosby, who was the complete antithesis of the kind of hunter who lives to kill. For over twenty years he had been coming from Minneapolis to hunt with Bert for a great ram to the point of making an annual pilgrimage of it. Time and again he had passed up chances to take good rams, for he wanted a very special kind of trophy—a huge old buster of a ram close to the end of his life trail.

He generally hunted with us alone. Over the years he and Bert had become very close friends, a fact soon apparent to me upon my joining the outfit. My role on these expeditions was that of horse wrangler, packer and apprentice guide. I was warmly aware of being accepted and welcomed by these men as a third member of the party, invited to trail in the hunting and given full credit for my ability with horses and knowing how to climb. If there was one thing I had trouble understanding, it was the philosophic, easygoing and enormous patience. Time and again they looked over good rams and turned them down without a flicker of disappointment showing on their faces. Neither of them seemed to mind if the bag was empty at the end of a long trip; they just planned another. Being young I did not realize at first that they were enjoying themselves just looking, not caring a whoop if anything was shot; something that comes with experience and savoring good company in hunting camps scattered across the Rockies. Sometimes I wondered if we ever would find a ram that would get these two excited.

Then came a day in September, delightfully cool and clear, when the three of us topped a ridge above timberline to glass a deep basin below very much like this one. Lying prone on a natural overlook among some scattered rocks to hide our heads, we combed the place thoroughly through three pairs of the best binoculars until I was personally sure that I had minutely examined every boulder, clump of brush and tuft of grass not just once,

but at least three times. Although some of the trails on
the talus fans at the back of the basin looked dark and
sharp cut as though from recent use, not a living thing
was in sight.

A big lone billy wandered into view around a shoulder a peak above. I gave it a cursory glance or two, but
we were not interested in goats.

Then Bert grunted and got to his feet to lead the way
out across a wide open stretch of steeply pitched mountain meadow covered with bunch grass. We had gone
about fifty yards single file, when he suddenly dropped
as though shot between the shoulder blades, and we
came down flat behind him an instant later. I could hear
Bert swearing softly and fluently to himself and knew
he had seen something mighty unusual. Then my eye
caught a flicker of movement in the bottom of the basin
about seven hundred yards below amongst a mess of
boulders. Slowly turning my head for a better look
through the glasses revealed five rams—all real patri-
archs, and then I knew the reason for the swearing. All
five were big but the largest was an animal to stop the
breath. He was big all over, a deep charcoal grey, and
his mahogany brown horns were massive, swept well
back in the curls and coming around in a full swing
with the broomed tips about even with the bridge of his
Roman nose.

How we missed seeing them earlier is still a profound
mystery to me, for they were in plain sight, though
bedded deep among the boulders. I could have wept, for
here we were pinned down in the open like a trio of rank
greenhorns, and it looked like we would have to stay
anchored till dark or the sheep decided to move. Every
eye was fastened on us, and as big rams will often do,

"What goes on here? Just that photographer again."
INSET: *A bull elk competing for graze on the winter bighorn range*

Free climbing is an art, taught me by Bert Riggall—and duly passed on to my sons

One learns where to draw the fine line between safety and peril, and never makes mistakes

The goat loves to lie in a rocky niche looking out across a valley

A mountain goat in the British Columbia Rockies

BELOW: *Mountain goats live far above timberline most of the time*

Dall rams in the wilds of the Yukon mountains—unmolested and unafraid

In the southern Alberta Rockies, recording with cameras the lives of the bighorns

A fine trophy bighorn ram shot with the camera at thirty yards

BOTTOM: *Bighorns in a carefree frame of mind*

Walter Lonker on the dream hunt of his life

A man who catches up to a goat in this kind of country earns his trophy

Franklin Crosby looks down almost sadly at his great ram

The author hunting with a camera in goat country

BOTTOM: *They don't come much bigger or more handsome*

A typical Dall ram—king of the Alask and Yukon mountains

A bighorn ewe, showing the sharp-curved thrusting horns

A young, three year old bighorn ram

they did not even bother to get up on their feet. Then the big herdmaster rose to give us a long hard stare, but when we did not move, he lay down again, calm and serene.

I had the taste of bitter hopelessness in my mouth feeling sure we were beaten without a hope of doing anything about it. Incredulously, I heard Franklin Crosby chuckle softly to himself behind me, obviously amused at the joke that was on us. It was almost more than I could stand.

But Bert had other things in mind. Hissing to get our attention, he softly told us to slip out of our rucksacks and jackets, prop the bags up against anything handy and drape our jackets over them. He set his packsack up against a little tree about two feet high, wrapped his jacket around it and then tied a red bandanna to the tip of the tree above, where it swayed and fluttered in the breeze. Motioning for us to keep flat with our noses in the grass roots, he squirmed downhill into a bit of a trough leading back and down at an angle to a tongue of shintangle scrub. We trailed along wiggling like snakes as close to the ground as we could get. It was slow going and a long crawl. When I finally dared sneak a look at the rams, they were still bedded down with every eye still fixed on the beguiling flag Bert had left behind.

It is amazing what hard work such a crawl can be even when downslope, and by the time we reached the screening scrub and could sit up, we were wringing wet with sweat. Fifty yards farther and we were in heavy timber, where Bert led off at a trot straight toward the rams. Finally he slowed to a walk again to lead the way out to the edge of a meadow for a quick look. He nodded at our hunter with a smile, took the shoulder-high alpine stock he always carried and placed it cross-wise across a gap between two branchy pines to make an improvised arm rest. Beckoning to Franklin to sit down behind it and take his shot, Bert lifted his glasses to watch.

Through my binoculars I could see the big ram a bit beyond and up the slope from the rest. He was lying broadside but a bit quartering towards us with his eyes still fixed on the decoys. Our friend took his time to steady down, then aimed very deliberately and fired. The bullet popped on the rocks throwing up a puff of dust six inches low. It was a long reach for the little 7 mm Mauser, close to three hundred yards, with the ram seeming to offer a much bigger target than he really was, for we were looking downhill at him. At the shot, he leapt to his feet and bounded a few jumps straight away up the slope at an angle to come to a stand looking straight away with his rump patch showing white against the dark grey rock.

"Hold right between his horns a foot over his tail," Bert murmured softly.

As calmly as though he was in a shooting gallery, Franklin Crosby chambered a fresh cartridge, aimed and fired again. This time the unmistakable plop of a bullet striking flesh came back to our ears. For a second the ram stood motionless, then turned slowly downhill weaving on his feet to suddenly collapse and roll over dead.

We were jubilant as we made our way across to the ram and Bert whooped when he got a close look at the horns. This ram was truly a buster—big, burly and fat. Our friend had collected a trophy of a lifetime, one of the biggest and oldest I ever saw killed. It was the one having sixteen annual rings on its horns allowing one for broom-

ing, and as sure as we stood there in our boots, we had
witnessed a master sheep stalker at his best, improvising
and making use of his knowledge of sheep and available
cover.

Now Kay and I were confronted with a similar prize
but a different kind of dilemma. We had plenty of cover
leading directly to the rams, but we dared not use it, for
if we tried, the rolling and eddying wind currents would
most certainly give us away. Our best and only chance
would be to circle wide and come down on them from
the top of the buttress ridge above them, so we headed
for our horses. While the hurricane roared I led the way
in a great circle down and across the valley below picking
a circuitous trail through the heavy timber. It was a bit
hair-raising here and there when we heard the thunderous crash of a big tree coming down. Striking a heavy
elk trail, we made better time across the bottom and up
the far side. Finally we rode into a comparatively
sheltered spot amongst a scattered grove of larches in the
lee of a knoll. There we tied the horses and proceeded on
foot. At timberline we came out among some low scrub
and swung down at an angle over a steep slope to a bench
overlooking the place where we had seen the rams. On
hands and knees we crawled out through a belt of
scrubby fir and sat up for a look. The rams had vanished.

Very carefully examining every foot of ground
through my glasses, I finally spotted the top edge of a
big curling horn showing over the rim of a gully. The
rams were lying in the bottom of the wash just beyond
out of the wind. With rifles ready, we waited for them to
move. Perhaps half an hour went by, when a puff of wind
must have blown down to them from above giving them
our scent, for they suddenly exploded into view heading

straight up the mountain on the dead run past us. The big ram was in the lead.

"Take him," I said softly.

Kay aimed from a sitting position while I watched to spot her shot. But nothing happened and when I looked to see what was wrong, it was to see her frantically taking the safety off. She had been trying to shoot with it on, something never too good to calm the nerves. Now the rams were at our level and passing like racehorses at about one hundred fifty yards. Kay shot but her bullet went a good foot behind the ram's tail powdering rock in a puff of dust.

"Shoot before he gets behind those rocks," she implored.

Picking the ram up in my sights I swung with him and fired, but the steep angle fooled me and my bullet went under his belly. Now the rams were flying and I committed an error. For a fraction of a second I looked down at my rifle as I bolted another cartridge. In that short interval a ram just behind the big one took the lead, and without even looking at its horns I swung my rifle past its nose and killed it stone dead in mid-stride.

The instant I pulled the trigger, I knew I had shot at the wrong ram. "Damn if I haven't killed the wrong one!" was all I could think to say. "Quick! Take him!"

But the rams had gone behind a rock spur and when they reappeared they were about three hundred yards away. There they all stopped to look back bunched up close together with the big one standing a bit to one side.

"You can anchor him there," I told Kay. "He's the one on the left."

"But I might wound another one," Kay said. "No, I've missed my chance. Let's let them go."

I did not argue, for the choice was hers. Besides she was smiling and unconcerned as she watched the sheep running in a string across a sheep trail on a talus fan towards the far side of the basin.

We dressed out my ram, propping it open to cool. I piled some brush over it to keep off eagles and magpies, then took the head down to the bottom where I hung it in a tree. Climbing back to our horses we headed for camp planning to come back with a packhorse in the morning.

Next morning it was snowing a blizzard out of the north and the driving wind had the cold dry smell of the arctic in it and the feel of winter. I found the horses humped up, cold and miserable, in a patch of timber a mile or so down the creek from camp, brought them to the rope corral and caught a couple. Kay wanted to come with me but I knew what it was going to be like at timberline, and persuaded her to stay in camp.

Leading a packhorse I headed out. It was a wild day at timberline with flying snow sometimes cutting visibility to fifty yards. By the time I reached the ram, skinned it out, cut it up and packed it, there was a foot of snow on the ground and it had turned mean-cold with no letup in the wind. When I reached camp in late afternoon, the warm tent was welcome.

By the following morning it had almost stopped snowing but the sky was lead grey and the temperature away below zero; so we holed up to weather out the storm. The tent was warm and cheery and there was plenty of wood to keep it that way. We had brought some good books and Kay had some wool for knitting. She alternated between reading, getting meals and knitting me a pair of socks, while I cut wood, kept track of the horses and took my turn at the books. Once, I rigged up my fly rod, much to her amusement, went up the creek to a beaver pond and cut a hole through the ice with my axe. Using a wet fly, jigging fashion, I soon had enough fat cutthroat trout for our supper, although my line froze solid in the guides of the rod.

Watching her knit as she sat in a comfortable improvised chair, while the fire crackled cheerfully in our sheet iron stove, I had the wonderfully satisfying feeling of knowing a remarkable woman. If either one of us had been shading some opinions about the other, they would have come out during that three day storm. Being stormbound in a mountain camp was not new for us, but this was the first time we had shared one alone. There is not much of importance two people can hide from each other in such a spot with the wind moaning cold among the trees and peaks; no friction between personalities that can remain secret, for this is the supreme test.

It was the beginning of a long, adventurous, sometimes worrisome though happy trail called marriage. Like all people we have had our share of troubles, but when the chips are down these fade to nothing and we can still look at each other and smile after nearly thirty-five years.

If I were to design a coat-of-arms for our family, it would feature a mountain flanked by a grizzly and a bighorn ram, for our tracks have been entwined with theirs and the mountains have been our home and talisman from the very beginning.

7

Mountain Hunting Today

The mountain hunter is a specialist; the one to whom hunting is usually more than just going forth to kill something, for these individuals have an almost obsessive passion for the game. The wild ranges where the peaks stand tall and craggy, their domes and pinnacles sometimes glittering with ice and frosted with snow, make pictures carried back to civilization in the mind's eye—something that pleasantly and permanently infects the blood. The true mountain hunter is willing to sacrifice much time and hard work in pursuit of his sport, for just reaching the hunting grounds often necessitates the mounting of an extensive and expensive expedition, well planned and organized. It matters not if he is a Johnny-come-lately or a veteran, the means he finds to attain the end may take a good portion of his life, so he may be on the sunset slope of his years before his dream comes true and he finds himself pursuing the wild ones among the crags with legs that have seen better days.

There was Franklin Crosby, who was still a young man when his trail turned towards the pursuit of big-horn rams, and who was such a purist that he hunted simply for the sport and really did not care if his annual pilgrimage to the Rockies ended in an empty bag.

When he finally killed the great ram that had been the grail beckoning him all those years, he was looking back on sixty-six winters. I recall him standing thoughtfully watching us prepare the big head for taxidermy. For a long time he said nothing, and then more to himself than to us he remarked, "Sheep hunting has kept me young. In a way I regret shooting that ram, for looking for him has been the excuse for coming. If I quit, it will likely be the finish of me." He sounded a bit sad, as though he had momentarily been given a glimpse of the future; but then he smiled warmly and was his old self again.

Although none of us realized it, his words were prophetic. That was his last hunt. Through circumstance, he was unable to return and, true to his prediction, passed away two years later. Somewhere in the home of one of his descendants there hangs a great ram's head, a fine example of the taxidermist's art, a sort of talisman preserved to remind those that see it of a great man who was touched by the magic of the little red gods that dance and cavort in mountain campfires.

A mountain billy is easy to stalk if you get up to his level or above him, perhaps the easiest of all mountain game to collect, if one leaves out of account the nature of the terrain he occupies. He has excellent eyes, probably just as good as those of sheep, and is very capable of making himself very scarce if he chooses, but rough ground offers lots of cover and unless one is very careless about the wind, getting a shot at reasonable range is not difficult. Sometimes the mountains do not cooperate. I have always classed this game as being among the most dangerous, not because he is apt to attack with his stiletto-sharp horns, but simply owing to the perpendicular pitches of the places a billy calls home. It is the kind of terrain where one careless step or bit of bad judgment can put a man over a drop-off on a swift journey of no return.

One occasionally finds goats where all that is necessary is to step off your horse and shoot, but this is the exception. Most of the time the saddle horses are tied up to trees at timberline, and the stalk is carried out on foot.

There was a time when a hunter and I were approaching a fine billy in a traverse along the face of a steeply pitched strip of talus trapped between two cliffs with a thousand foot sheer drop below. What would normally have been a very easy stalk was complicated by a foot of snow. It was crusted and dangerous for there was a skiff of loose new stuff on top. So I was well in the lead scouting out a safe route and then beckoning my hunter to come up to me, where he would wait for me to go ahead to the next point. It was slow going and working well until I walked out on an apron of glare ice hidden by the new snow. Instantly I was glissading towards the top of the cliff below, still on my feet and in control although unable to stop.

A hundred feet below and a few feet ahead there was a strip of bare rock whipped clean by the wind, and I knew if I could hit it without losing my balance, I could stick. But to do this I had to curve my descent. Braking hard with the tip of my climbing staff and pitching the edges of my boots, I managed to make the turn and came down on the rough rock. When I stopped I could look down for a long way into a boulder field.

Standing where I had left him about three steps short of the ice, my hunter was looking down, his face a study in utter horror and fright. He was as safe as if in church where he stood, but he was a mighty scared man. Talking to him quietly and telling him not to move, I worked my way up around the ice and back to him.

Looking at me as though I had returned from the dead, all he could say was, "My God! I thought you were a goner!"

Meanwhile the billy we had been stalking had seen me make the slide and was fast legging it up the sheer face of a cliff into an impossible place as fast as his feet could take him, so we set about getting out of there back the way we had come. By this time my friend had about the worst case of the shakes I have ever seen. He shivered and shook from head to foot. Even his teeth were chattering as though he'd just come down with a very bad chill. It was slow and patient business getting him down off the face of that mountain, and by the time we reached our horses I was a mighty tired man. Reaction had set in by that time and I was completely drained, but a stiff shot of hot rum laced with butter and honey back in camp set us both up again to something more like normal.

A couple of days later we made another long but much easier climb and collected the billy. No doubt every time my friend looks at that trophy on his wall, his mind does not dwell on the shooting but on a climb we made along the slope trapped between two cliffs.

Another danger goat hunters sometimes face is avalanches. A heavy fall of snow will occasionally avalanche off steep faces, a development that can be deadly for anyone caught below. However, avalanches are not too difficult to avoid and there is really not much excuse for getting caught in one, for rarely will goats or other game be found where one is ripe for falling. Wild animals sense the danger, but occasionally the quarry will be in a position to toll hunters across dangerous terrain as they approach.

The late Norman Luxton, an old acquaintance of mine and the founder of the famous Luxton Museum in Banff, had an experience one fall while hunting goats that was whisker-close to being his final one.

He and two of his friends were out in late October stalking a bunch of billies across a talus fan. There was a cliff fifteen hundred feet sheer falling away below and the rest of the mountain above and a foot of powder snow underfoot. Norman was behind his companions as they traversed a normally very easy and safe slope, when suddenly a dry slide let go somewhere above.

A dry snow avalanche can be a triple danger, for if you miss being buried or swept off a cliff, you can smother by breathing the flying powder snow accompanying it. The stuff gets into the lungs and melts, simply drowning the unlucky one.

Norman and his friends heard the slide coming and could see the great rolling cloud of snow coming down towards them and began running to get out from under it. In seconds they were blinded by the fog of powder snow and crouched down to bury their heads in their jackets. When the slide went by and the air cleared, the two leading hunters found themselves alone. They looked for

Norman, but he had completely disappeared. The slide had passed very close before plunging off the cliff below and they sadly concluded he had been caught in it and was lying somewhere far down the mountain, dead, for nobody could survive such a fall.

More or less in shock, they retraced their steps. Being experienced mountaineers, they were sure there was no chance of finding Norman alive. It was a long way to the bottom and darkness caught them before they could make a search so they went to camp. There they built a fire and dug out the bottle of rum for a stiff toddy. They did not feel like eating, but they did have another drink. That one led to another as they discussed the sad demise of their partner, and somehow the night resolved itself into a kind of wake for the departed one.

But Norman was not dead. Caught in the slide, he had been swept over the lip of the cliff, but lodged in a little scrubby tree growing out of a crack in the rock just under the rim. Knocked unconscious, he had been hanging there covered with snow and his partners had missed finding him. After dark, he regained consciousness to find himself suspended over nothing, and somehow managed to crawl to safe ground above. One arm was broken and he was battered and bruised, but he was a tough and determined man. Guessing why his partners had left, he slowly and painfully trailed them down the mountain under a late moon to camp.

Meanwhile the bottle had been emptied and the fire had gone out. The two mourners had crawled into their sleeping bags for warmth and were lying there suffering the depths of utter despair, while a couple of candles burned somberly lighting the inside of the tent.

Then from the night outside came the sound of

groans in the distance and they thought they heard a voice say something.

"Dear Jesush!" one of the mourners exclaimed. "If I was a shuperstitious man, that would shound like a ghosht!"

"Must be the wind," said the other.

But the sounds came closer accompanied by the crunching of feet in the snow, and then the tent flaps parted to reveal Norman tottering on his feet, splattered with dried blood from a deep scratch on his face—returned from the dead.

"Where is the goddam rum," he gasped. "I need a drink!"—the understatement of his entire lifetime.

Shocked into complete sobriety, his friends helped him to a seat, and built a fire all the while trying to explain why there was nothing left to drink. At first they had trouble convincing Norman why there was no rum, and when the fact got through to him, he became utterly furious, berating them for a couple of profanely described idiots. A pot of hot tea served to calm him down a bit and they attended to his arm.

They finally got him back to Banff and a doctor, and in due course he saw the funny side of the experience and forgave them. To his dying day Norman proclaimed goats the most dangerous game in the world.

I recall corresponding with a banker from Kansas one time, a man who had worked hard all his life to realize a dream big game hunt in the Canadian Rockies. When he finally persuaded himself that he could afford it, he was in his late sixties and booked a trip with me. Knowing he had been harnessed to a desk chair for a long time and was likely in pretty soft condition, I persuaded him to take a three-week packtrip and come alone.

He followed my advice and upon meeting him I was glad, for he was in much need of careful conditioning. Should a guide overlook a hunter's condition and proceed to take him too fast and too high on those first days of a hunt, it can result in much disappointment for all concerned, and even danger to the client.

Once in my own experience one of my clients suffered a coronary attack during a climb, and within seconds of getting a shot at an enormous billy. My head guide and old friend, Wenz Dvorak, and my son Dick were with him and had maneuvered a very polished stalk to intercept the billy as he came down off a high mountain wall to water. Wenz was in the lead with the hunter a step or two behind him as they approached an outcrop where the goat would be within easy range. Suddenly the hunter gave a sort of grunt and fell headlong into a patch of salmonberry brush. Both guides thought he had just tripped and fallen, but when they came to assist him, they found he was dead.

No doubt, the unaccustomed exertion at high altitude plus excitement and a heart condition he had kept secret, all contributed to his death. Although the incident involved the usual nerve-wracking consequences, it was a good way for a man to go; for what better way for a hunter to die than suddenly within rifle range of a great trophy on the face of a craggy mountain, the sun bright on the autumn colors of the lower slopes and a gentle wind whispering along the cliffs?

Although a general license allowed my hunters to legally kill seven or eight head of game, I had placed a camp limit system into practice, allowing each client four head for any given hunt in a single season. Besides being very selective, this kept my territory well stocked, for I limited each season to four expeditions and each hunt to a party of four. It was not a way to get rich fast, but it preserved a way of life and assured the satisfaction of knowing my activities were not hurting my wilderness hunting grounds. This cropping of trophies was somewhere under the normal mortality from old age among the game, taking into consideration the kill of resident hunters, mostly after meat. It served to help keep the game population within the holding capacity of wintering grounds—always the basic governing factor in any big game country.

All this I carefully explained to my new client, Walter Lonker, and being a banker accustomed to balancing books along with knowing the necessity for reserve funds, he could readily see my reasons. He agreed to my suggestion that we hunt the easier game at lower levels first. I would take him very carefully through his first week on the trail, showing him the many sidelights and explaining the host of fascinating things that go with a wilderness hunt. As his legs and wind improved we could go higher for the sheep and goats he wanted.

It was fun hunting with Walter, for he was like a boy on his first visit to a circus; everything interested and delighted him. He was uncommonly lucky too, for on his second day out we were sitting in the shade of an old trapper's shack eating lunch at noon, when a great thrashing and crashing suddenly came from a patch of willows across the clearing fifty yards away. Our horses began snorting and dancing around the trees where they were tied. I picked up Walter's rifle and handed it to him just as a behemoth bull moose stepped out into view. It was the beginning of the rut and the bull had his wires crossed, for he was showing unusual interest in our horses—something that occasionally happens. Walter was visibly shaken by the size of the animal and I made him hold up on the shooting, talking to him softly while I eased him into a comfortable position. When he had calmed down a bit, I told him to go ahead and collect his moose, which he did with a single shot through the neck. As we looked over the bull, Walter was fairly dancing with excitement. He had good reason to be pleased for he had opened the hunt with a fine trophy. The bull was big all around—it took three big packhorses to handle the meat and head.

The weather was perfect for a fall hunt, and over the next ten days we wandered on horseback among the mountains keeping to lower ground with some short climbs into basin pockets we could approach in the saddle. Walter collected a fine mule deer on one of these trips and a glossy black bear on another, neither of which he had ever seen in the wild before. Two or three times I scouted alone up into a region where bighorns are sometimes found, trying to locate a bunch of rams. But it was marginal sheep country at best, and none was found. So on the final week of the hunt, we concentrated on getting a goat.

This, of course, meant taking Walter up onto the high slopes, which I did with care. For although he had toughened some, he was still a long way from the man he would have been twenty years earlier. There is just no way one can fully compensate for the erosion of the years.

Having spotted a fine billy lying in a pocket on a cliff face within a hundred yards of the cover of a rock spine dropping down the side of a high ridge to timberline, we were not faced with anything like a difficult climb. Even so, we went with caution, and I took every excuse to give him plenty of time without making it appear I was leaning over backward to make things easier for him. He handled himself remarkably well, and after a couple of hours we reached the billy's level well screened by the rock rib.

Climbing ahead to a vantage point, I found the goat had got up to feed along a wide ledge and was double the range away, but the shot would be still an easy one for Walter's neat, flat-shooting .270 rifle. Getting him into a comfortable position, we waited for the billy to turn broadside, whereupon Walter fired. The bullet went high, hitting the rock beyond in an explosion of dust. The billy whirled and jumped back towards us, coming about fifty yards before it stopped again. This time Walter dropped him in his tracks—a good thing, because he was within one step of the cliff edge where he would have fallen and rolled a thousand feet, likely breaking his horns.

"Good shot!" I congratulated him.

"Should have had him the first time," Walter replied. Then he added, "But how do we get to him?"

Up to that moment I hadn't really paid much attention to the location. It was a fair kind of question, for the goat's ledge was just under a smooth perpendicular cliff from twenty to fifty feet high that ran along the mountain for a considerable distance. The ledge was blind at our end where it butted into the dike under an overhang at our end. Beyond it petered out to the next thing to nothing—good going for a goat, but not the kind of place where one would enjoy packing out a trophy skin, head and meat. Besides, this route would add up to a long way around.

Telling Walter to stay where he was, I climbed out

along the top of the cliff over the goat where a steep dry wash came down, working my way down to where a water-worn pocket overhung the ledge ten feet below. Using the same trick Bert Riggall had taught me years before, I lowered myself over the edge facing the mountain and dropped to land on my feet facing out in another similar pocket.

Skinning out the goat and cutting up the salvageable meat was routine. Then I carried it to a spot directly under where Walter sat watching the whole operation. Instructing him to get a length of sash cord out of my rucksack and climb down to the top of the overhang, I tied the meat and skin in two packets with some string carried in my pocket. Walter came down onto a ledge very gingerly and lowered the end of the rope. In no time he had pulled the meat and skin up onto the ledge.

When this was done, he looked down with a worried expression and asked, "Now how do you figure on getting up here? Sprout wings, maybe? This rope isn't strong enough to hold you, and I can't anchor it here if it was."

"Give me time," I told him. "It may take me a while, but if I'm a bit late, you have plenty of meat for supper!"

A bit beyond where the goat had been lying I had spotted a crack in the rock leading up to the top of the cliff. It was narrow and tricky, but it might do. Free climbing is always easier for me going up, perhaps because it is easier to see what one is doing. Reaching up and working a hand into it, I found a finger hold and hauled myself up to where I could jam a boot toe into it and then reached up with the other hand to locate another hold. It was a matter of raising myself on my arms for the toeholds were little more than something to steady me. In a couple of places the inside of the crack was smooth, so I just closed my fist to lock it in and make use of the friction to lift myself. This kind of thing is painfully rough on the hands and it was a relief finally to squirm over the rim and stand up.

When I reached Walter, he reached out to shake my hand. "Some show! What a grand finish to a great hunt!" he exclaimed. "I will never forget this day!"

That is the way such a hunt should be—pleasantly unforgettable. A good hunter-guide relationship is always warmhearted, a kind of mutual sharing of the fun and appreciation of each other's feelings and skills. The guide who looks down on his hunter as a green and ignorant dude not only takes the joy out of the game, but is being foolish and unfair. He is overlooking the fact that he would also be out of his element in the hunter's home environment; and if he had to make a living in those surroundings, he would be shown up for a wet-behind-the-ears individual doomed to failure. By the same token, the guide who considers the kill to be the hallmark to fame and fortune is overlooking a very big and important part of the game; namely, satisfying and knowing how to keep a hunter happy even without tallying a big score of trophies.

I remember one trip we had with a trio of young fellows on their first mountain big game hunt, in which they all killed their limit of rams and goats before ten o'clock on the first morning. It was one of those unusual and highly rare circumstances where we just fell into a situation making the bag possible. But the hunters were not impressed. It was too easy, and although every trophy was excellent, they lost interest. Two of those hunters never came back. As far as I know they never went big game hunting again.

Personally, I have developed a philosophy that if I could place a man—no matter who he was or how he felt about killing a game animal—within range of a good trophy, it mattered not a particle if he killed or not. One way or the other, I could still count the score in my private tally book. Never have I berated anybody for missing, or made him feel I was disappointed. What a man did when I put him in range was his business. To the man, my clients responded favorably to this approach to the game.

I remember spotting a fine trophy billy one bright October morning from the cook tent door in a snug camp at the bottom of a deep narrow valley in British Columbia. I pointed it out to my friend, Harry Jennings, and we decided to climb for him, although he was almost at the top of a high mountain.

Harry is a man with a built-in love of mountain hunting and wide experience ranging from stalking Dall sheep and caribou in the Yukon to trailing goats, elk and grizzlies down in my old hunting country. He is the sportsman's kind of sportsman, and before he retired was also one of the most skilled heart specialists in Canada's medical circles. In his own quiet, unassuming way, he has been one of the finest rifle shots I ever knew on both targets and game. He could afford good weapons and could use a rifle with skill under all kinds of conditions. I never had the feeling of being a guide while out with him, just a companion and friend privileged to enjoy his company. We rambled the mountains savoring many things, sometimes taking a trophy, but just as often passing up an animal after looking it over.

This particular stalk was made early in our acquaintance and was a kind of milestone in a long friendship. We climbed a long way over a steep slope out of bare rock into snow halfway to our knees into the teeth of a wintry breeze. Finally about noon we came up onto a spur below a castle-shaped buttress of rock. When we reached the top of this, we would be within two hundred fifty yards of the billy.

My leg muscles were tingling and I knew Harry was tired; so I suggested we eat lunch. Leading the way around into a sheltered place against a sunlit face of rock out of the wind, we ate our sandwiches and enjoyed our pipes. Then we climbed to the top of the rock buttress above. When I peeked over the skyline, it was to see the billy standing on a pinnacle exactly where I expected to find him.

He was a venerable old goat with his fall pelage heavy and thick; his pantaloons and beard waving gently in the wind. Standing broadside, he was a beautiful and unforgettable picture against the deep blue of the sky. Pushing my rucksack up onto a rock for an armrest, I signaled Harry to go ahead and shoot when he was ready.

He slid into a comfortable position, quietly sliding a cartridge into the breech of his rifle. I had my glasses up waiting for the shot, knowing just as surely as I stood there in my climbing boots that the goat was ours. Nothing happened and when I looked at Harry again, he was straightening up and opening his rifle breech.

Grinning at me, he asked softly, "Why should I kill that old fellow? I've already got a good head on my wall. What I came out here for was to get away from my telephone! Chalk one up for us."

The last we saw of that goat he was still standing there completely oblivious to our presence, gazing away off into the distance. We climbed back down to camp and a warm fire knowing the good feeling of having enjoyed a great day in the mountains.

A good mountain guide has to be a sort of jack-of-all-trades: horseman, packer, naturalist, climber, gun expert, field medic, and diplomat. It is good if he also is somewhat of an entertainer too, when bad weather ties everybody down and slack time can get heavy on the hands. Furthermore a bit of well-timed showmanship once in a while does no harm, adding some spice to flavor what would otherwise resolve into sheer boredom.

While all the above-mentioned attributes of a wilderness guide are desirable, probably the most useful and desirable is diplomacy. It can smooth out rough spots and make living a lot more enjoyable. What is mountain diplomacy?

There is a story told about two Irishmen walking a mountain trail through a rabbit jungle of lodgepole pine. Paddy, who was in the lead acting as guide, pushed into a small broken-off snag hanging chest-high across the trail, springing it away around to the absolute limit before it snapped back and popped his partner squarely under the nose.

Hearing Mike's cry of distress, Paddy looked around to see him sitting on the trail with blood streaming down the front of his shirt. He apologized by saying, "Begorra! I'm sorry. I should have been more careful."

Getting slowly to his feet and looking at Paddy through his tears, Mike assured him, "Sure now, Paddy, it's a good thing you hung onto it! The son-of-a-bitch might have kill't me!"

This is the exercise of mountain diplomacy.

8

Being Your Own Packhorse

In the old days many of the early trappers and prospectors who explored the interior of British Columbia and the Yukon went by means of their own two feet carrying their food and equipment on their backs. It is a tough way to travel but has its advantages, for it allows a man to go where there is no horse feed and through country where the rivers are too swift for water craft.

Fifty-odd years ago R. M. Patterson made an epic journey north from the Peace River to the fabled Nahanni River of the Yukon, spending months exploring the great canyons above and below the magnificent Virginia Falls. He was looking through the country called Headless Valley, so named because a party of prospectors disappeared there one winter, and later, when their skeletons were discovered scattered about in the vicinity of the rags of their tent, the skulls were all missing. A story of mysterious murder and intrigue was born. The real explanation is thought to be much less dramatic, for no evidence of foul play was ever found. The missing skulls are more likely explained as having been rolled into the stream by investigating bears and lost forever. However, the more sensational explanation remains a subject of much controversy.

Patterson spent most of a year rambling through the region discovering caves, hot springs and a host of other interesting features that make this unique area one of the most interesting in North America. When he came out, he brought with him a collection of photographs as well as notebooks crammed with material later incorporated in his book, *Dangerous River*.

Lord Tweedsmuir, at one time the Governor General of Canada, and a famous novelist who wrote under the name John Buchan, wove the story content of his novel *Sick Heart River* around this same fabled wilderness. In it he featured a backpacking wilderness traveler. His research was done firsthand, for he visited the Nahanni River country when it was little known in the company of Harry Snyder, the famous hunter and explorer. They were the first party to fly into the valley. It was on this expedition that Snyder discovered and hunted in a magnificent range of mountains just north of the river— mountains that now bear his name.

Many of the early prospectors involved in the Klondike gold rush were no strangers to backpacks of various kinds. Some carried unbelievable loads up over Chilcote Pass in the dead of winter. A great-uncle of mine, a tough Scot by the name of Neil McTavish, carried his food and possibles over trails reaching thousands of miles from Colorado to Alaska and northern British Columbia in his lifelong search for gold. I recall sitting around the fire in the evenings with him as a boy listening to the stories of his adventures, little realizing how much work and hardship had been absorbed by his tough, powerful body. He was near seventy then, but still straight and strong, his kindly face weathered by desert sun and arctic storms and laugh wrinkles curving away from eyes accustomed to looking across miles and miles of mountains. He died when well over eighty in a little town called Smithers up on the Bulkley River in northwestern British Columbia, still looking for the pot of gold at the end of the rainbow.

Backpacking in those old days of trapline and prospecting trails was not nearly as comfortable as it is today with modern pack frames designed with scientific precision and balance to fit one's back and shoulders. When I first packed my gear on my back on trapline forty-odd years ago, the best equipment we could get was the Bergen Pack, manufactured in Norway. The bag was hung on a triangular tubular metal frame supposed to fit the wearer's back. I have a long back and never found one really comfortable on a long haul with a load. Inevitably I came in off such a trip with one thought uppermost in my mind: for the simple reason I hurt in a number of places, how wonderful it was going to be to get that load on the ground—definitely the first thing to be done regardless of anything else that might be waiting.

My feeling about packs has a kind of parallel with a story told about two Finnish soldiers skiing back from the Russian front to their home towns during the hostilities early in World War II.

They had been fighting on skis for months and were heading home across country, a journey of days and tough winter camps with a minimum of grub. Finally they topped a big hill looking down on their village, and

paused there to savor the peaceful setting and the anticipation of warmth and food.

The older of the two men asked the other, "What is
the first thing you are going to do when you get down
there?"

"You know I was married just a few days before we
went to the front," the other replied. "I haven't seen my
wife for three months. The first thing I am going to do
is fill up on one of her wonderful stews. Then I am going
to take her to bed for a week!" Then he asked in turn,
"What is the first thing you are going to do?"

"The first thing I am going to do is take off these
goddam skis!" came the positive reply.

Dissatisfied with the packs available in trading posts
and outfitting stores, trappers began improvising their
own. I recall being loaned one such pack frame made with
two broken ax handles and quarter-inch iron rods for a
trip in northern British Columbia. It was a comfortable
pack and it was designed with enough strength to with-
stand the trampling of an elephant, but it weighed
enough to be a pretty fair kind of load without adding a
pound of anything else. It was thus the modern pack
frame was born. The first really practical and comfortable
pack I ever used was the Trapper Nelson design constructed of light canvas stretched with lacing over a
light basswood frame on which a roomy bag was hung.
It was a kind of pack saddle for human use, a vast im-
provement in its time, for it was light, protected the
packer from any hard projections of equipment in the
bag and weighed only a few ounces.

It worked well in winter, but had its shortcomings
for summer use. In warm weather there was little ventila-
tion between the canvas and the wearer's back, and it

could become scalding hot. I found out all about this uncomfortable drawback one summer in the Yukon.

The incident had some unique aspects, for after years of working with broncs, climbing and traveling wild country without so much as cracking a bone, I fell through a scaffold while shingling my house and broke several ribs. Our family doctor taped me up with copious application of adhesive to the point where I had trouble breathing. Shortly after I took off on an expedition into the wilds of the western Yukon and during the course of events began climbing every day with a load of motion picture equipment. The weather was hot and in due course I began feeling exactly like an old, well-worn packhorse with a badly fitted saddle and a skimpy saddle blanket. My back began to itch and burn to an intolerable degree. Late one afternoon, my sons, Charlie and Dick, and I arrived back in camp dragging our shirttails after a long tough day in high country. My back felt like somebody had poured coal oil over it and struck a match to it, so I pulled off my shirt and instructed my sons to remove the tape. This they did while I ground my teeth in agony, solemnly promising myself all the while that I would have some pointed conversation with my doctor on the shortcomings of using tape for correcting broken ribs plus some earthy comments on his ancestry thrown in for good measure.

The tape came off. Along with it came pieces of hide and bits of meat, for we found I had a whole assortment of little boils under it. The boys swore they could see into me clear to the bone in several places, but I suspected they exaggerated a bit for their own amusement, although I felt like the sun was shining clear through me. They swabbed off the raw places with a soft, clean handkerchief soaked in overproof rum, an operation which almost made me howl, and then rubbed in some bacon grease. In due course my back healed up and I have looked with deep compassion on every horse I have seen since with saddle sore marks on his back.

There is nothing like such personal experience to make a real impression on a man, and nothing more inclined to make him look for improved equipment. Owing to the demands of mountain climbers, hunters, hikers and specialized military forces, outfitting firms designed and experimented with various combinations of light but strongly constructed pack frames made of aluminum and magnesium alloy tubing. There are many kinds, but the best has emerged in a type known around the world as the Kelty Pack, which incorporates about all the most favorable features of everything ever invented in the line plus some innovations of its own. It is a comparatively expensive piece of equipment, the frame being constructed of feather-light magnesium alloy tubing and coming in four sizes to fit anyone. It follows the contours of the back, riding on wide bands of nylon webbing which can be laced to varying degrees of tension and insure that nothing can rub the wearer. A kind of padded bow rides over the packer's hips, and this is secured by a strong belly band, to avoid tipping and swinging when climbing. On the frame is slung a well-designed bag with inner compartments and outside zipper pockets for food and possibles. If one packs his gear so that heavy items ride fairly high on the shoulders, the balance can be adjusted to afford easy carrying. With the inclusion of a well-designed nylon mountain tent and a down-filled sleeping bag, it is possible to keep the load well under fifty pounds and still be reasonably comfortable for a couple of weeks. Of course one must take advantage of the very light, freeze-dried foods that are available in many combinations. This kind of combination is a high-country sheep hunter's dream come true, opening up a whole new horizon for the modern cameraman or hunter working country too rough for horses to negotiate.

Backpacking on a hunting trip for any kind of big game has its definite limitations. It is a specialist's way of going, and the "specialist" had better be in reasonably good physical condition. In any event, it is wise to take it easy for two or three days to give his muscles and feet a chance to tone up. It is profoundly important that his footgear be comfortable and afford the very best protection for the feet.

No backpacking hunter will ever likely be accused of being a game hog, for his bag will be confined to one animal and that nothing heavier than a mule deer, goat or sheep. Even then he must be prepared to relay his meat and trophy out to more sophisticated transportation. Game such as moose and elk are out. A bull elk or moose is one of nature's most impressive animals on the hoof, but to kill one and then stand contemplating the inert mass of hide, flesh and antlers, knowing that it had to be carried out piece by piece on a pack frame of any kind, could be one of the most discouraging experiences of a hunter's life. Personally, I prefer shooting such animals with my camera to take the trophy home on film, then buy a side of beef. Any other way, the price of meat per pound gets unbelievably high before the job is done. As an Indian once remarked, it is much easier to camp by the moose and eat it where it falls.

After a lifetime of rambling through the mountains of Alberta and British Columbia with horses, I now find

myself slinging a pack over my shoulders when I want
to enjoy the remnants of what was once a vast wilderness
of sheep country. It is the only way I can recapture the
feeling of great freedom and spiritual rest that was once
an everyday way of life. By climbing high up into the
remote pockets and high basins, where cliffs and canyons
defeat the persistence of the wasters, it is possible to
camp beyond the sound of motors, where the air is sweet
and clean as the mountain streams and the peaks look
down across mantles of shining snow. I miss the cheery
sound of Swiss bells on grazing horses and wonderful
camaraderie of equine friends, but sometimes at night I
still hear them, faint and far off, lying snug in my down
robe with the smell of spruce and pine in my nose.

Every fall a young rancher and friend, Billy Morton,
and I take off for a week of sheep hunting. We are very
choosy, for while we have seen many sheep, we still have
to find a suitable bighorn ram for him. He carries his
rifle, but I go armed only with a camera. At first he was
keen as a sharp hunting knife to kill a ram, but as time
has passed he has become more and more the hunter for
hunting's sake. Someday he will kill a ram, but when he
does, I suspect he will feel a bit let down and wish perhaps
that the search was not over.

Two years ago we drove his four-wheel drive up a
creek along an oil prospect road to where a deep canyon
cut it off not far from where I once camped in the old
packtrain days. There, we left the vehicle and took off on
foot. We climbed up over a mountain shoulder and down
into a beautiful timberline basin just under the cliffs of
the Continental Divide, where we set up our little mountain tent. From there we hunted the country up and down,
then picked our outfit up and moved on to new ground.

It took us most of a week to comb out country that could easily have been covered in half the time with horses. We ate smoked venison saved over from the preceding fall, cooked our meals over a tiny fire and washed in ice cold streams. The weather was bad with snow flying on the wind like winter and ice forming on the creeks sufficient to carry our weight. Our climbing boots were wet for days. We saw sheep, will-o'-the-wisps grazing high among stringers of fog and snow, but none with heavy horns. Three times we climbed to over eight thousand feet above sea level. Almost every night we dragged ourselves into camp after a long day of tough climbing in bad footing. But we enjoyed it, for there is a challenge to that kind of hunting like no other. Billy gained experience he could get no other way. I had the satisfaction of knowing that in spite of half a century of trails behind me, I could still ramble through high country when conditions were about as tough as they could get.

It is thus that a man can reacquaint himself with old familiar ground and relive the satisfaction of traveling along the rugged flanks of the shining mountains far from the ant heaps of noise and dirt we humans call civilization.

9

By Packtrain in Wild Sheep Country

Back between 1950 and 1960, what had been some of the finest mountain wilderness in the world for horse travel was torn open and desecrated by oil and mineral exploration companies with roads and seismic lines cutting it to ribbons. It was a particularly sad thing for us to watch, for we were intimately acquainted with about every square yard of the area lying between Banff and Waterton Lakes National Parks, and then west to the Flathead River. With the exception of one small piece of magnificent mountain wilderness in the extreme southeast corner of British Columbia in the Flathead River drainage system, it was all gone, chewed up by the much-lauded "multiple use" program which the politicians claimed was fair, because by this programing everyone is supposed to get the opportunity to enjoy the recreational and natural resources instead of only a few. In reality, the only people that made any profit from the trade were the oil, timber and coal interests. For a while the new road systems afforded fishermen and hunters bag limit bonanzas, but then the success ratio sank with sickening speed.

At first, very few people knew or cared about the fact that any given piece of country can only stand so much industrial pressure before the environment is damaged to the point of yielding only a fraction of its normal production. Nobody realized that prevention is vastly less costly than repairs after the damage is done—even if repairs are possible, which is too often not the case. To mess up a piece of country beyond redemption is easy; restoration is extremely difficult and sometimes impossible. Mountain country above timberline in the Canadian Rockies is a sub-arctic ecosystem extremely sensitive to mechanical pressure of any kind.

We had known the mountains when the only way to get into them was on foot or by horseback, when limitations of time and mode of travel put the governor on access. Overgrazing by domestic stock was the first major damaging intrusion, but this will heal itself with time and adjustment. As late as July, 1960, while guiding a family from Princeton, New Jersey, we had ridden through and counted over four hundred elk and a hundred bighorn sheep without really looking for them in a piece of country about three easy days long by packtrain up on the headwaters of the Oldman. Later that same year we conducted two successful hunting trips in the same region, but while the time lapse could be counted in days, we could see swift changes.

John LoMonaco and his wife Barbara were with us, and their prime interest was bighorn rams, but forestry and prospectors' helicopters had driven away all the sheep. So we turned our attention to elk, which had just taken shelter in the heavy timber when the planes flew over them. Barbara killed a fine bull, but our luck was bad as we tried to find a matching one for John.

On the last day of the hunt, the weather was warm and windy, not the best for finding elk, but we proceeded to make a big circle up through some high basins for a last look for sheep along the front of the Continental Divide. After eating lunch on a ridge top overlooking a great stretch of old burn, we swung down and back towards camp over lower ground through a scattering of dry muskeg and parkland meadows.

We had completed about two-thirds of this circle when we came to the edge of a big swamp covered with scrub birch, willows and grass—ideal elk country. Stopping the horses on the edge of the timber on a slight rise of ground commanding perhaps fifty acres of open ground, I reached for my call. Pulling a fair-sized piece of mountain air into my lungs, I blew a challenge only to have it muffled and blown away by the wind. It seemed hopeless to try to make it carry any distance and it was doubtful if a bull elk three hundred yards away could hear it. Because there was nothing better to do, I waited for a slight lull in the wind and blew it again.

Then our ears caught an answer somewhere upwind, resonant, deep-toned as a pipe organ and stirring; the unmistakable bugle of an old bull. Then it came again from the direction of a hollow about one hundred fifty yards upwind and out of sight inside a screening grove of lodgepole pines. Then just over the top of a swell of ground at the edge of the trees my eye caught a flicker of movement, the ivory tips of antlers gleaming in the sun, top royal points of incredible length and spread. They rocked slowly and majestically in timing with a measured stride and as the bull came slowly up a gentle incline more points were revealed until finally the whole animal was in view.

What a magnificent bull he was, big, slab-sided and strangely marked with silvery blotches. Quietly I told John to get ready. Here was one for the book.

John was an experienced hunter, but when he took a look at that bull he came about as close to falling completely apart in a case of buck fever as he likely ever will. He fumbled his rifle out of the scabbard, jammed his glove on his right hand as he tore it off, and took twice as long to get into shooting position as he normally would have. By this time the bull was crossing in front of us scarcely a hundred yards away, an unbelievable sight in the fall sun. His antlers were incredibly large and formed —six long points to a side, double curved in the beams and symmetrical. The brow tines came way down even with the end of his nose; one turned up in normal fashion, the other bent down, likely from getting caught amongst the herbage as he fed when the antlers were still soft in velvet.

"Six points to a side," I told John in a low voice, trying to sound calm and nonchalant. "Nice trophy. Take him."

John lifted his custom-built, scope-sighted magnum .300, with which he could hit a six inch bull's-eye at two hundred yards and missed the bull broadside at less than half the distance. Unaccountably, the bull paid not the slightest attention, continuing to walk, proud, arrogant and utterly magnificent. With a visible effort, John got hold of himself and hit him just back of the shoulder about halfway up the ribs. The great animal stopped, turned slowly in his tracks to stand looking at us, regal and wild. Another bullet slammed into him and with a great sighing grunt, he tottered and fell.

When we reached him I stood amazed. For not only was this the biggest elk ever killed on the outfit, but his hide was close to a golden palamino color adorned here and there with silvery spots. Sometime previously, the bull had been in a fight and his adversary had apparently put a tine of an antler in his mouth, then twisted it out through a cheek, breaking the lower jaw. The bull could drink but had been unable to feed and was slowly starving to death. Its body was big but very gaunt—almost emaciated. The unusually marked cape was not damaged beyond repair by the horn wound on the jaw, but the meat was unusable.

When I skinned out the cape and lifted the big head across my saddle, the tips of the antlers swept the grass on each side of my tall horse. Tying a stick across it back of my saddle cantle to hold it up, I lashed it down securely and then carefully led my horse back toward camp. John and Barbara trailed behind grinning like two kids, happy with the prize.

Later, while we stood admiring the trophy lying on the ground in front of the tents, I told John, "It's a pretty fair substitute for the ram we didn't see." And then added, "It's also a pretty good way to wind things up. This is the last packtrain hunt I will be taking in this country."

John looked at me with an expression that spelled disbelief and concern, asking, "Do you really mean that? What's wrong? This country looks mighty good to me."

"By this time next year," I told him, "there will likely be a road up this creek right where we are standing. You have written the last line to the final chapter. Not much point for anyone to hire a packtrain where they can take a taxi."

As it turned out, I was right. That grand country on the headwaters of the Oldman, a region of so many happy memories, is gone; torn up and left in broken shards, a place where one is rarely out of sight of bulldozer tracks and too often still within sight and sound of the machine that makes them. So a family tradition that had begun away back in 1907 when Bert Riggall had led the first packtrain expedition into this part of the Rockies became history. We sold most of our outfit and I turned my attention towards trying to save something of what was left of the western Canadian wilderness, for the call of wild country was still strong.

During the years that followed my trails led me far north way down across the far Arctic, where the vast sweeps of tundra lie like rich green carpet unrolled between the ranks of snow and ice-capped peaks. There thousands of caribou, moose, Dall sheep and bears still wander the wild free land. It was a fascinating time full of action and adventure in places where the great quiet of the north was often an almost tangible thing one could feel seeping into his bones—an aura of peace with a quality beyond words to describe. Sometimes when I stood looking out across the miles or lay snug in my robe at night beneath pale stars, I had the momentary feeling of something missed. It was a fleeting thing generally broken off by something that took my mind elsewhere; but I knew what it was, I was lonesome for my horses.

Several times over the next few years, the family rounded up the horses we had left and we took off on trips into the mountains with the cameras through Waterton Lakes Park into British Columbia. Even though this region was still comparatively remote and wild, we were oppressed by the knowledge that even this was slowly being eroded away.

The people who made their living in the park providing service to visitors were succumbing to the lure of the sound of cash registers. For example, one ambitious businessman came to the superintendent's office with a letter from a visitor of the previous year exclaiming that he wanted to come back with his family because, of all the parks he had visited, this one had an aura of peace and quiet that was irresistible.

"We should use this in publicity for the Park!" the bright-eyed Chamber of Commerce member bubbled enthusiastically. "Think of all the people who would enjoy our peace and quiet!"

When it was pointed out to him that that quality did not go with crowds, he looked baffled and somewhat hurt as he retreated.

The good members of the Chamber of Commerce were pressing for a highway running west and south linking Waterton in another direction with the country to the south through this last piece of wilderness. And by their blindness threatening the quality of peace and quiet they extolled. They dream of more motels and camps and more blacktop roads; a place where the unbroken ballad of ringing cash registers paves the way to heavenly happiness. They do not look up at the rams feeding on the slopes or the ewes that need wild secluded places to have their lambs. They do not worry about the harried grizzly, whose very future is threatened by the lack of wild country it must have to exist. They do not even think of their own comfort or that of the people who would flood into the place. For certainly the additional disturbance would upset the fine balance of the wilds—a condition where the pendulum of balance would swing away over and stay stuck on the side of commercial greed at a point of no return. There would be no place in that picture for quiet camps snuggled down on the edge of green meadows by clear, pure streams and the protection the parks were designed to afford wild species would be a mockery.

Because of such problems my thinking was beginning to change; for as a naturalist with a long-time, built-in concern for animals, birds, fish and the many other facets making up the complicated life patterns of this country, my awareness of people was growing beyond just obdurate resistance to their pressures and blindness. The thought took root and grew that only through understanding and management of that complex animal known as man, could we be assured that bighorns would always walk the talus fans and ridges and the great clawed tracks of grizzlies continue to be printed on ground and snow. Only by bending the blind selfish wills of the spoilers and persuading them that they too would fully share the losses, could we hope for cooperation in necessary management. For a long time we had been mighty short on foresight, or we might have done something to stem the tide with time less pressing and comparatively more minds less atrophied by the lure of fast profit.

Although I knew very well the frustration and the discouragement of bucking so-called progress and the complacence of those who did not care, I longed to go back into the mountains again with horses where it was big, wild and free, and see it with more perceptive eyes.

There was still some big country left where horses were used up along the Continental Divide of northeastern British Columbia by outfitters giving service to sportsmen from all over the world. It was not nearly so easy to reach or as hospitable as the country we had known so well, but I yearned to go for a look.

It is a strange thing how the minds of two men, complete strangers, living thousands of miles apart can reach out through a common bond of interest and thus come to know each other, ultimately become friends and share the joy of rich experience. It is an illustration, rich in relatively untapped possibility of what might be done if men give free rein to their better qualities, thus find the full measure of communication available to us in this age of electronics, fast transportation and the realization that we all share what has become a very limited earth-neighborhood.

At the same time I was wondering how to get up into northern British Columbia on horseback and see some more unspoiled country, there was a man sitting in a richly appointed law office in Fort Lauderdale, Florida. On occasion at the end of a long hard day he dreamed of big wild country—big country he had never seen—far from telephones and the pressures of law courts. I did not know it then, but on such occasions he would reach up onto a shelf and take down a book titled *Grizzly Country*, and thumb through it, momentarily losing himself in vicarious wandering through the mountains. The book was very familiar to me because I had written it.

Then one day there came a good letter signed, Gene Heinrich. It arrived among others from strangers, for a writer gets many communications from those who read his work and are moved enough by it to take the trouble to write. So far I have tried to answer them all, although it adds up to a lot of hours. Occasionally one comes that rings the bells in one's consciousness of a truly common bond of interests, however great the distance involved or the diversity of making a living.

He wanted to go on a sheep hunt, he told me, and added that he was not a very experienced hunter, had never been in truly wild country, but wanted to try it. He did not necessarily want to kill a big trophy, only a typical specimen; mostly he wanted to see and get to know something of the mountains with a good outfitter where sheep lived. Did I have any suggestions?

I offered to get in touch with a reputable outfitter and set up arrangements for a first class wilderness hunt. He in turn invited me to join him for the two weeks I was able to arrange with Leo Rutledge, North America's top horse outfitter, located in northeast British Columbia.

So it was one bright sunny morning we loaded our gear into the baggage compartment of a Piper Aztec on the blacktop apron in front of a hanger at the Fort St. John airport and took off. In a few minutes we were flying north along the twisting yellow ribbon of the Alaska Highway with a checkerboard of farm fields under our wings for a short distance and then the vast stretches of green bush. Mountains lifted their craggy heads off our port wing and on the starboard side the sinuous river valleys wound their way northeastward to the distant horizon; bushland as far as the eye could see.

As the props chewed the air and the engines droned, the country became rougher and the mountains closer. Now the blue sky was darkening with clouds and when we banked away west of the highway, we were crossing the wide valley of the Prophet River above its fork with the Musqua, where these rivers join to wind down northeast past Fort Nelson on the first leg of the long journey to the mighty Liard and Mackenzie rivers ending in the Beaufort Sea.

The pilot jockeyed our craft deftly through rough air over the ridge crests towards mountains that grew higher as the overcast pressed us down. Then we slid back into the valley of the Prophet heading into weather looking anything but good, for rain squalls hung in ragged canopies between the peaks, and sometimes the blackening cloud cover hid their heads. It is these clouds with hard centers that pilots avoid like poison. We flew through a narrow gap over a gorge where the river was torn to whiteness by a series of cascades and falls, and then came roaring into a wider stretch of valley low over spruce timber. The pilot swung and banked the plane over a strip of meadow where we could see a snug camp set up close to the foot of mountains flanking the valley. This was Leo's headquarters camp, he told us, but the strip was about three miles farther up the valley where the horses would be waiting.

I was riding the co-pilot's seat and could feel my belly muscles tightening as we flew on westward, for rain was streaking the windshield and the weather thickening. There was nothing in front of us looking like a landing strip to me. Dead ahead a solid wall of limestone loomed through the rain coming closer and closer. We were letting down with the tops of the spruces flashing by close under the wings. Then there was a willow strewn flat beside the stream and beyond a gap through the timber. I looked and thought, we can't possibly be landing here. I shot a look at the pilot. He was intent but calm and undisturbed as if he were landing at his home airport. The plane settled a bit, slid through the gap in the trees and came down towards what looked like a moose pasture with an orange wind sock flying from a pole alongside.

Gravel crunched under our wheels and we came to a smooth stop on the wildest-looking airstrip I had ever seen.

Leo Rutledge, tall and lean, his strong weathered face smiling a welcome, came over to greet us as we climbed from the plane. In no time, our gear was up on pack-horses snugged down under diamond hitches, and Leo's crew were busy introducing us to our saddle horses. When I looked them over, I knew this was an outfit that knew and cared for horses; for they were sleek and contented-looking and the gear on their backs was the best.

It is always something of an occasion to meet a new saddle horse one has never seen before, and this was no exception. A young broad-shouldered redhead dressed in blue jeans, mackinaw shirt, well-worn chaps, and boots, all topped off with a jaunty hat, walked up to me leading a big brown, slab-sided gelding. I took the reins and we looked each other over, both of us noncommittal. Booting a stirrup I stepped up on him.

"His name is Chocolate," Bob Walsh told me as he threw a leg over his saddle. "He's a good horse."

I had his word for it but I wondered as we fell into line heading for camp, for Chocolate was going at a dis-interested walk, shuffling along as though all his joints were coming unhinged.

Lifting the reins a bit I told him softly, "Look, you big raw-boned son-of-a-bitch! You're not packing a green-horn dude! I've eaten bigger and tougher before break-fast!" I kicked him gently in the ribs to punctuate it.

Instantly his head came up and his ears lifted. He looked back at me, his eyes brightening as though an inner light was snapped on, and he broke into a long flow-ing walk as smooth as silk. Chocolate and I had started to get acquainted and my spirits suddenly soared.

We were following the trail along the edge of a flat through some willows, when up ahead along the line a bronc ridden by a young Indian horse wrangler spooked at something and went sunfishing out to the side bucking hard. His rider stayed for a few jumps, then went flying on his back into a willow clump to the huge merriment of the rest of the crew. Somebody caught the horse and the butt of the fun got back up in the saddle with a wry grin to ride back onto the trail.

Just ahead of me, Bob opined dryly, "Hell of a way to celebrate, getting bucked off!"

"He didn't buck off," I remarked. "He just lost his hat and then got off to look for it!"

Bob's shoulders twitched in silent laughter, and right then I felt absolutely wonderful. I wanted to cut loose with a war whoop of sheer joy, but decided the dignity of years could pass without it. Sure as the sun came up in the morning, this was a trail outfit. It was good to be home again.

Leo's camp was an attractive, semi-permanent affair located on a flat where a side creek came down past a limestone dome, the mountain where the famous Chadwick ram was taken. In the middle of the flat a long low commissary and cook shack was built of plywood over a stout frame with a spring piped into it for water and gas from portable propane tanks for cooking. It was presided over by a couple of efficient ladies who fed us like kings. The bed tents were pitched around the edge of the flat and a big horse corral was located on a bench by the creek. Most of the camp had been flown in piece by piece over the mountains.

As we rode into camp, the sun came out lighting up the whole country, and we sat our saddles looking back up the valley at a backdrop of high limestone peaks; the main range of the northern Rockies fronted by a bright rainbow hanging over the green timber.

A couple of days later we cut out twelve head of horses from Leo's bunch including seven packhorses, four saddle horses and one for a spare. Leo had everything we needed for two weeks carefully packed in matched pairs of pack boxes, each pair balanced to the pound. The balance of these boxes, which are slung on each side of the horse, is most important and can mean the difference between easy going or trouble, a happy horse in contrast to a miserable one with a sore back. Packing up a trail outfit for a wilderness trip is a process requiring meticulous attention to everything from grub items to the smallest piece of equipment, for to be out on the trail for even two or three days without something like a simple can opener can be a nuisance and aggravation that can only be endured.

The packhorses are saddled carefully with plenty of padding under the rigging—good big clean blankets with no hard spots or wrinkles. Pack saddles vary considerably in style and the way they are rigged. Some outfitters use the southern-style Decker rigs, the kind originally developed for use by the old American cavalry for packing heavy, odd-shaped objects. The trees of these are hinged to automatically adjust to the shape of an animal's back and have heavy pads built into them, and are generally fitted with two cinches, a breast collar and a crupper. Most of the outfits in the Canadian Rockies use the common, and less adjustable, wooden sawbuck saddles. Some are double-rigged, others have a single cinch with a breeching to keep the load from sliding too far ahead and a breast collar to hold it from slipping back.

Almost every outfitter of experience has his own special variations in fitting his saddles and throwing the hitches. My own favorite rigging employed the sawbuck saddles equipped with a single cinch, crupper and breast collar adjusted to fit every horse. Each saddle had the horse's name to which it belonged branded on it to avoid getting them mixed up, for each had its straps set with about two inches of play where the crupper went under the tail and about four inches at the breast collar. It is important to have the breast collar loose enough to allow the horse to put down its head without shifting the load forward. This simple rigging was the result of many years of trial with all kinds of variations and we had a minimum of trouble and breakage with it. Many a time we traveled all day with twenty horses carrying from one hundred eighty to two hundred twenty pounds apiece tied down on these rigs without having to adjust a single pack on the trail.

Some outfits tie their packhorses together in strings of five or six animals apiece to be led by various members of the crew. This method has definite disadvantages in rough terrain, for a horse can get jerked off balance in a tricky place. We never led our horses, but trained them to follow a lead horse. It was quite a sight to look back down a long string of loose packhorses and riders winding their way along a sinuous trail through timber or on an open skyline—sometimes forty to fifty animals all carefully picking their way over extremely rough ground.

Each pack is fully made up on the ground with the boxes loaded and top packs of sleeping robes, duffel bags and tents matched to them. Care is taken not to have the top pack too heavy, for otherwise it tends to swing and may overbalance the pack. Each load has its canvas mantle made of heavy duck material, about five by seven feet in rectangle, to cover it keeping out rain and protecting the pack from snags.

Sometimes the boxes are fitted with straps or rope loops by which they are hung from the crosstrees of the saddle, but more often they are hung by use of a basket hitch tied with a rope. Then the top pack is put on with the mantle laid over all and neatly tucked in all around. A lash cinch fitted with a hook at one end and a ring at the other to which is attached a forty-five-foot soft manila rope is used to tie the diamond hitch lashing the whole load to the horse. Putting such a load on a snaky bronc can sometimes be a trying business, and gentle horses are a boon to any packer. But if the load is put on properly, with adequate rigging, it will generally stay.

Trying to tell anybody how to throw a diamond hitch is about as impractical and impossible as attempting to write instructions for playing the violin. It just can't be done, for it is something best shown firsthand and then practiced until mastered. It is not enough to just have the words and the tune, one must have the method of application. Sometimes the diamond is thrown by one man, but it is better done by two, with one working on each side of the horse. There are several variations, all very ingenious but simple when you know how: the half diamond, three-quarter diamond, diamond and double diamond. Bert Riggall and I worked out yet another variation, the Riggall pot hitch, an almost foolproof method of tying a cylindrical and slippery top pack down on our cook boxes. As far as I know, no other outfit ever used it. In throwing the diamond or any version of it, no rope ends are ever pulled through, and it can perhaps be best described as a big double bow with the loops caught under the boxes and the loose knot pulled out in a diamond shape on top.

Two men who know their business can average about four minutes a horse, thus packing up a string of twenty horses in an hour and twenty minutes. If the loads are heavy, two tons of gear can be involved, and, as I have heard an old packer say, all it takes is a strong back and a weak mind.

In a competition at a horse show one time, Dave Simpson, my foreman, and I packed a horse using the basket hitch and diamond with full gear starting with everything but the saddle loose on the ground and then ran a hundred-twenty-five-yard course with our saddle horses and the packhorse in one minute thirty-seven seconds. It is a record that has never been broken and likely never will, for experienced packers are getting few and far between. Another time for exhibition, we packed a horse while blindfolded, the pack passing the inspection of a competent contest judge. All of which gives some idea of what long practice can do.

Leo's crew were experts and in short order we were on the trail. We had Bob Walsh for cook and Danny, a northern Cree Indian, for guide. Our trail led us up a creek coming down out of the high country past Chadwick's mountain. At first it switchbacked up through spruce timber and then traversed slopes tangled thick with alders and willows. A mile or so farther up we climbed into typical tundra country, where the trail swung and wound up a big open valley towards a pass among some lesser mountains. Here and there caribou moved through the scrub willows.

We nooned at the top of the divide between the Prophet and Musqua rivers with vast stretches of tundra-covered plateaus and ridges stretching away below us. Across the Musqua to the north, range upon range of high mountains cleaved the sky. The sun was warm and a zephyr of breeze stirred the tails and manes of the horses as we headed the outfit down the talus slopes.

That evening we wound in along the foot of a high craggy ridge to pitch our tents in a grove of big old spruces overlooking a sweep of grassy valley. This was truly wild country occupied by caribou, occasional moose and numerous stone sheep with very little to disturb them. We had seen rams looking down at us from the skyline as we traveled, and we could hardly wait for morning.

At sunup Danny brought the horses into camp and we caught our mounts. Danny was in the lead when we rode up the valley west of camp flanked by craggy ridges on either side. Almost immediately we began seeing stone sheep, mostly ewes and lambs, but within a mile he spotted rams high on the slopes among some chimneys and broken turrets. A long look through the spotting scope proved them to be young ones with only one mature specimen in the bunch. His horns were nothing to get excited about, so we left them grazing and moved on up over a pass following a faint trail down the far side. This was mighty big country with miles and miles of slopes to glass, a place where time went by with amazing speed.

It was mid-afternoon, when we tied the horses to climb on foot around a mountain spur to look into a rugged side valley. It was spitting rain when we reached a look-out point commanding the head of this canyon, and the peaks at its far end had their heads wreathed in grey mist. As usual there were caribou scattered far and wide, some of them high amongst incredibly rough country. A big bull was bedded down on a saddle on top of a shoulder with wide velvet-covered antlers etched black against the sky. Two more big ones looked down from a perch where one would expect to see rams on top of a steep buttress sticking out like the gable of a church above us. Everywhere we looked caribou moved or just lay resting.

Then near the head of the valley below us my glasses picked up something moving and a moment later a fine ram led his bachelor's club out of a clump of willows beside a white-water creek. There were six of them and the leader was a very handsome ram with a black cape and white ringed muzzle, trim, well muscled body and a fine set of horns forty inches or better on the curl. They were in a playful mood, alternately displaying their heads and spinning in circles gamboling as carefree as lambs. They took turns butting heads in mock fights, although this was mid-August, still months from the rutting season. At irregular intervals they would all go trooping back into the willows by the creek, and I wished we could see what was going on there. Then again they would suddenly reappear as though on parade to go through another session of play. There was no way we could approach them without giving them our wind, but it was enough just to lie there watching them. Gene was enthralled, for this was his first good look at mountain rams.

As we put away our binoculars to turn back toward our horses after an hour or more of watching, he said to me, "If I never shoot anything on this trip, it was worth coming just to see those rams! What a sight! They have got to be the most beautiful animals that walk the face of the earth."

Something of the setting and atmosphere of this kind of country puts a man in a frame of mind where he sees and feels things never experienced anywhere else. The spruces around our tents were big, jug-butted old trees; many of them eighteen to twenty inches through at their bases tapering quickly to their tops forty or fifty feet high. In such climate this was heavy timber, as big as trees ever get in this sub-arctic land. Counting the rings on the stumps of dead ones we were using for firewood made a man realize they had been standing there for centuries overlooking the valley long before white man ever saw the country. As near as could be told without special equipment, the biggest ones had been growing there for at least seven hundred years.

The tents overlooked a small creek winding down a shallow valley about half a mile wide sloping down off some wider flats near its head. It was a kind of corridor between high limestone ridges with spines and turrets lifting along the rims. To the north another spur stretched away several miles indented with steep-walled basins along its flanks and below these giant terraces and plateaus fell gently away to the rim of the canyon overlooking the Musqua River. This was typical northern alpland where timberline is about twenty-five hundred to three thousand feet above sea level; tundra country in the higher reaches. Except for some scattered spruce groves and low willow and birch growth mixed with sweeping meadows around a couple of small blue lakes, there was not much timber growth compared to country farther south. Most of it was covered with abundant feed for game. It was no wonder Leo's horses looked sleek and fat, and obvious why we were seeing so much game almost everywhere we looked.

Lifting up back of our tents was a rugged mountain flanked on the east by a saddle. Beyond this Danny told us there was another series of deep valleys too steep for horses, but where big rams were often found. We would go look into it, but it would be a backpacking proposition.

So we loaded up some grub and our sleeping bags on pack frames and started out. Almost immediately upon getting onto the rim of the saddle back of camp we saw sheep, but all females and lambs with a few young rams scattered among them. The narrow, almost invisible trail slanted steeply down over broken scree on the far side to some boulder fields and mountain meadows at the head of a wild valley. Then it twisted up losing itself here and there among more boulder fields to the top of another pass.

By noon we had come several miles, mostly up and down, and were stretched out in the warm sun resting tired muscles and fortifying ourselves with sandwiches and candy bars. Danny was with us, but Bob had stayed in camp to keep an eye on the horses. We were nooning on top of a tundra-carpeted, little plateau with an immensity of mountains stretching away for miles in all directions. A man could spend months looking through this country without seeing it all. Some of the peaks soared to well over nine thousand feet, reminding me of the grey limestone mountains farther south on the old hunting grounds on the headwaters of the Oldman and Highwood rivers, except for the many glaciers glittering in the sun. Above the thick spruce growth along the bottom of the steep-sided valleys, the heads of the creeks were folded and benched in innumerable pockets and ravines—all prime sheep and caribou range.

We prowled around from one look-out point to another sweeping the country with binoculars and spotting scope in search of rams; but none were in sight.

Mid-afternoon found us climbing down a mile-long slope pitched steeply into the head of a twisted timbered canyon, where a white-water creek tumbled and brawled its way among big boulders toward the Musqua River. Down there at a fork of the creek Danny told us a cache was waiting where we would camp for the night. Gene and I were aware of leg muscles begging for rest, for there are few things that wear on unconditioned muscles like carrying a forty pound pack down such a slope over bad footing. Shintangle scrub tore at our legs, loose rock rolled under foot, and when we came to timberline it was to find ourselves toiling through thick moss up to our knees, the heaviest growth of this stuff I have ever seen. It was like walking down over a thick feather mattress. Some open bare rock gullies invited us to quit this wallowing and climb down over the cliffs and shelves, but going down over such a place on tired legs with a load was too dangerous, so we stayed in the timber and toughed it out.

With only twenty-three years behind him and constant exposure to this kind of country to make him whale-bone tough, Danny was as tireless as the rams we hoped to find. I watched him picking trail in the lead remembering the time when I too knew what it was like to be like rawhide with no limit to the miles. I thought of Chocolate back at camp and envied his holiday. But finally there was an end to it and we came out along the creek.

Picking our way up over the water-worn boulders was a relief after that slope, and a quarter of a mile upstream we came to what was left of the cache. It had been hung on a crossbar between two trees in waterproof sacks and contained a tarp, some blankets and dried food; but a grizzly had made use of deep crusted snow the previous spring to reach up and tear it down. It was a total wreck, but the loss was of no real consequence, for we had brought food to last a couple of days. If we located a good ram there would be plenty of fat ribs to grill over open coals.

The moss made a wonderful mattress under our light down robes and a rough lean-to kept out the shower that fell during the night. Gene and I had no trouble getting to sleep, and it seemed we had scarcely closed our eyes before the morning sun was coloring the peaks and lighting up the tops of the spruces. We laced up our climbing boots while Danny busied himself over a breakfast fire crackling cheerfully on a shelf by an ice-cold little spring. He was his usual happy, carefree self as he tended frying pan and coffee pot and the smell of frying bacon and eggs made us ravenously hungry. He had all the best qualities of the Indian.

Out in their own country, far from the white man's civilization, these people are grand hosts with an outlook on life few white men understand and appreciate. They greet each day as the one posing the problems; tomorrow will be attended to when tomorrow comes. Like all humans, there are good, bad and indifferent among them. But to look down on them as a race with contempt because their ways are different is to advertise one's ignorance and lack of appreciation for their character and capabilities. To travel and hunt with them with an open mind is to realize how well they can manage with whatever is at hand. Danny, like his father before him, was a professional guide, hard-working, resourceful, proud of his record and very thoughtful of his companions. He was a master climber, a first-class hunter and fun to be out with.

While we ate breakfast, we planned the day's hunt. In order to cover all the ground possible, we would split up; Frank and I to climb up to a vantage point high above timberline, while Danny covered another. We would be in sight of each other most of the time, so if one of us spotted rams, we would signal and then join up for a stalk.

This being Gene's hunt, I was not carrying a rifle. When he and I shouldered our packs, I had a steep rocky ravine in mind for a route up onto the slopes above, not wanting any part of climbing back through the moss. Choosing one with a stream running down it, we worked our way up along ledges flanking the gorge—a spectacular place where the water leapt and plunged. Sometimes the going got steep enough to make us use handholds, but most of the way we climbed at a steady walk. When we came out above timberline, we could see Danny a mile away along the same slope in a spot where he could command some basins beyond our view.

It was pleasantly warm with a few fluffy clouds, and although this was August there was a smell of fall in the air. Here and there the scrub willow and birch was turning red and yellow, the first touches of autumn's paint brush. Never have I seen mountains more ideal for sheep, but for some reason or other they weren't there. We combed every chimney, gully, basin and rockslide repeatedly but could only find a few ewes and lesser rams. Meanwhile we could see Danny climbing up onto a ridge overlooking more ground, so we elected to follow.

We joined him at noon on top of a gently folded plateau. Again we were on top of a world of mountains, but still the big rams eluded us. We ate lunch in the warm sun using our packboards for comfortable back rests.

Gene was stretched out luxuriously and asked the world at large, "We seem to be where the rams ain't, but who cares?"

"Danny does," I told Gene, for I had just turned to

see him heading for a point of rocks with the spotting scope. "He never quits hunting. I swear he hunts in his sleep!"

A few minutes later Danny signaled us to come. He had found two fine rams bedded away out on the tip of a precipitous spur towards the Musqua. One was big with massive horns we judged would be close to forty-two inches on the curls. But the tips of his horns were broomed off a bit and Gene wanted one with perfect tips. Besides they were in a very strategic position, difficult to approach. The shot would be a long one, and unless the bullet was true enough to anchor the ram in his bed, he could fall half a mile. His horns might get broken and besides, it would take most of a day to get down and back up again with whatever was left of him; so the ram won the game without even knowing we were within twenty miles.

Picking up our packs we headed towards camp following a game trail down into a deep valley and up onto the high ridge on the far side. An old injury where a bronc had torn a knee cartilage years before was giving me a bad time. I was not lame, but just hurt at every step. Trying to save one leg tired the other and by the time I topped the second ridge I was in pure misery and mighty glad to be looking down at the tents.

But a night's rest did wonders and next morning I was back in the saddle fresh and feeling fine, ready to see some more of this vast country.

As we rambled up various valleys, sheep and caribou were rarely out of sight. The caribou bulls' antlers were still soft in the velvet but some of the racks they carried were impressive. Later in the fall their neck capes and flanks would be snow white, the antlers hard and polished as they competed for the females. Although the fly and mosquito season was about over, all the caribou were very high—many of them away up in the ridge crests above the sheep for the most part. Considering the width of the antler spread on some of the bulls we saw at skyline, mountain caribou are amazing climbers.

Many times we saw them crossing the valleys and as always I was amused and entertained to watch their reaction to our intrusion. Upon seeing us passing on horseback, they would give us a long look, their eyes bulging with an expression of incredulous amazement, whereupon they would hoist their stubby tails, give a lighthearted skip and go pacing away with that beautiful flowing gait so typical of caribou. For sheer poetry of motion there are few animals more graceful on the run, and certainly none so erratic and unpredictable.

Many times over the years when among caribou I have seen them stand rooted with curiosity. Then they will sometimes give a peculiar buck jump to go tearing off across country as though pursued by devils, only to stop again at any range from a couple of hundred yards to half a mile to look back still obviously burning with curiosity. Quite often they come pacing back to stand again a bare hundred yards away with their eyes big and round in a comic expression of utter disbelief, before again leaping away. At other times they run and never come back, as shy as whitetail deer. One hears them called stupid, but that is only relative to outlook, for human standards do not apply.

By the same token, I have often heard moose described as ugly, but again the description depends on the point of view. A cow moose undoubtedly looks fine to an amorous bull, and her calf extremely handsome to its mother.

As we rambled through the high tablelands between

the Musqua and the Prophet, we were seeing these animals too, huge and black in contrast to their surroundings, visible for miles. Here also one can only admire the incredibly graceful fluid action of their gait as they head out across rough ground. Never have I watched one without enviously wondering what it would be like to have one gentle-broke to saddle, for it would be a thrilling experience to ride one through the rugged country of their choice in the western mountains. They can go at twenty miles an hour where a horse would not dare set foot.

But Chocolate and I covered some wild rugged country. He was a big, strong, very cool-headed mount that seemed to enjoy my company as much as I relished his. Sometimes I rode him on scouting trips alone, and it was then his courage and independent spirit shone; for while he did not particularly enjoy being away from the other horses, he was always willing and very canny in his choice of trail over bad ground in swamps or steep country. Generally I gave him his head except for a general choice of route, trusting him to find a way that suited him best and thus getting us where I wanted to go with a minimum of stress. When I dismounted to use glasses or camera he never missed the opportunity to feed, always stayed close and never gave me a moment's trouble. Our association was very relaxed, and in spite of the fact that I rode him every day he stayed sleek and fat. Sometimes when we were miles from the tents and the sun was getting low in the west, he would give me a gentle nudge with his nose as though to say, "Hey boss! It's about time we headed for camp." And when I stepped up in the saddle, he would head out in that long silky walk with his ears up, happy to be heading home. Chocolate was one of the great characters of the equine world, trustworthy and tough—a horse of many virtues I will never forget.

Meanwhile we saw rams, but for one reason or another, Gene never fired a shot. But he was unconcerned, content simply to enjoy each day as it came, the hard work and sometimes vigorous weather. A natural-born sportsman and sheep hunter, he slipped easily and willingly into the pattern of patience, endurance; the finely drawn philosophic selectivity and sensitivity that is the brand of a good hunter loving the game for the sake of the playing. He moved from a position of some quiet unsureness to that of a confident, carefree man without a worry in the world. As the saying goes, he was one to ride the river with; shades of some truly great hunters I have known, and I, silently cheered him for it. The breed is anything but numerous.

But Danny was worried. Aside one evening, while we were unsaddling our horses after a long day of hunting, he turned to me and said, "I don't know about this man. He sure is particular. If we don't find him a ram I'm sure going to catch hell back at base camp. Nobody has ever come in from a trip with me without a trophy. We've passed up some good rams."

"Forget it," I told him. "You'll find him the ram he wants. But if he doesn't shoot one, don't worry about it. I promise everybody will know why." And then I added, "This guy is one who likes to save the frosting of the cake for last!"

Danny shook his head in some perplexity but grinned, once more his usual happy self.

Next day we rode out early in the morning west and north into a big valley some distance from camp that we had looked into but had not hunted. The place was crawling with caribou and heavy sheep trails crisscrossed the talus fans on both sides. As our mounts picked their way up a faint trail looping back and forth across bends of a busy creek, bunches of ptarmigan jumped out of the willows here and there under their noses. Small bunches of ewes and lambs stood on the slopes watching us as we passed.

We nooned on a bench with a grand view taking turns with the spotting scope to look over several bunches of rams up along the long ridge top opposite; but they were all secondary animals with horns that did not tempt. Leaving the horses tied in a clump of willows, we climbed over a high notch between two peaks back of us.

At the top of this pass we were looking down over a huge green basin at the head of a precipitous creek that fell away toward the Prophet through a snaky boulder-strewn canyon. We could see no sheep but had not gone two hundred yards before we found the fresh tracks of rams. The wind was shifty, forcing us to keep high on the near flank of the basin as we prowled from one vantage point to another trying to locate them. Somewhere in that jumble of ravines and hidden pockets was a bunch of rams. By just watching Danny as he ranged from one look-out to the next, it was obvious he was alert to a knife-keen edge but also frustrated. I could have sworn I smelled sheep on the warm damp wind, but look as we did, no rams appeared. Finally the setting sun forced us to climb back over the range to our horses.

Next morning we woke to find a blizzard driving across the flats in front of the tents on a steady northeast wind. Visibility was about two hundred yards and hunting conditions about as bad as they could get; so we stayed close to the warm cook tent and spent the morning playing cards and reading. But Danny was restless, and shortly left to get the horses. He wanted to go have another look for those rams. Gene was game, but I felt that on such a day as this I had lost nothing in those mountains. So Bob and I stayed to watch them ride away into the storm.

In early afternoon the snow gave way to rain, the ceiling lifting so the mountain slopes were in view near the bottoms, but up on top it was still a cold and forbidding-looking picture. I did not envy Gene up there among the flying willy-waws of swirling snow.

Bob and I played cribbage, swapped stories and enjoyed a leisurely supper. Finally we rolled up in our sleeping bags, thinking of Danny and Gene a long way from camp, siwashing it somewhere away off among the peaks around a fire in a clump of spruces.

Along about one o'clock in the morning I woke up. It was as black as the inside of a cow in the tent and for a moment I could not figure out what had roused me; but then over the sound of the wind and the sleet rattling on the tent roof there came a strange, weird kind of ululation lifting and falling, sometimes almost fading away and then coming back. Nothing I had ever heard in the middle of a storm on a dark night matched it. But then a lull came in the wind and the sound came through strong and clear. It was Danny and he was singing.

Pulling on my pants and boots, I went to the other tent and shook Bob awake. "Better get up and rustle some grub. Danny and Gene are coming and they've got a ram."

Bob must have been away off on some tropical beach

in mighty interesting company, for he was reluctant about coming back to life, and when he did he growled, "What the hell makes you think they've got a ram?"

"Listen! Danny's singing," I told him. "Nobody would sing on a night like this without some awful good reason. You can bet they've got a good ram!"

While Bob rattled and banged the stove, Danny and Gene rode up to the front of the cook tent, and sure enough Danny dropped a big ram head in the door. We turned a flashlight on it as Gene stepped off his horse grinning from ear to ear.

"What a hunt!" he exclaimed. "It was wild up there, but we found them—six good rams, and this is the best of the bunch. Man, I'm bushed, wet, froze and hungry enough to eat a boiled owl, feathers and all, but it was worth it!"

A stiff rum and honey toddy apiece and two big helpings of hot stew later, we got a running account of their hunt.

They had gone through a blinding blizzard up on the saddle leading into the basin we had looked into the previous day; but a little way down the far side they had come out of the fog and flying snow into slushy rain. Visibility was still bad, but they could see across the bowl well enough to spot six rams a half mile down the creek on the opposite slope up amongst some ravines and broken turrets. Back up into the cloud they went with Danny leading in a fast circle to get above and down wind from the rams. But when they reached a position to see the place where the sheep were feeding, they were gone.

Carefully, they hunted out three ravines, but found no clue as to which direction the rams had departed.

Nothing can swallow rams so thoroughly as a mountain with its head buried in mist. Because there was no use looking up, they watched the slopes below. About the time Gene had resigned himself to having spent some miserable hours for nothing, Danny pointed. Out from under a fold the rams came single file to cross the creek seven hundred yards below. Backtracking, Danny cut back downwind into the shelter of a deep gulch and then headed down the mountain at a fast pace, for the day was waning. When they reached the creek a long strip of willows afforded cover allowing them to come up to the place where the rams had forded. Careful searching revealed nothing in the first of a series of gullies coming in from the side, so they hunted the next. The long days of the past two weeks had hardened Gene but he was tired and discouraged when the first two draws showed empty clear to cloud line.

The third draw was full of brush at its bottom and their first look into it was fruitless. But then a feeding ram came up out of a dip at the top end of the willows. While Gene and Danny crouched motionless, five more came into view—one of them a picture book trophy. As often happens, the shot was an easy one and picking the right ram was no problem. Gene leaned over a big boulder, caught the big one in his sight and fired. The ram came tumbling down, caught himself for a moment and then collapsed.

As he told about it, Gene was again caught up in the excitement. He had every right to be exuberant, for next morning when I put a tape on the horns they measured forty inches on the curls—not the biggest ram in those mountains by any means, but a beautifully formed, truly classic specimen with perfect points on both sides. The cape was a handsome sooty grey and well haired out. It was a prize to cap a long hunt, and Gene was happy with it.

He was also sure that he had seen the ultimate in hunting and expressed the opinion that it would likely be his last hunt for sheep with a rifle. "Next time I come," he said, "it will be with a camera. Anything after this would be an anticlimax!" Then thoughtfully he added, "I hope the people in this country never let this place be spoiled. It should be kept just like it is."

As we wound back through the mountains towards base camp with our string of loaded horses, the sun was shining and the snow-capped peaks were shining as far as the eye could see in the crystal clear air. When we topped the pass looking down the long slopes towards Leo's snug base camp, Chocolate tossed his head and snuffled softly through his nose playing with the bit as I stopped him for a few moments to look down across the mile-wide basin moving with caribou. I too hoped British Columbians would break off their love affair with dams and mines and oil in time to set this country aside just as it was—a wilderness area like no other—a jewel to be preserved for the wild things that rambled through it—big enough and far enough back so hunting would never hurt it.

10

Exploring with Cameras

From the very beginning of my experience with Bert Riggall, it had been obvious that there were more ways than most hunters recognized to hunt wild game. He had shown the way to off-season stalking of all kinds of animals and birds with a camera; the trophies recorded on film often being more exciting to collect, and while the frying pan went neglected even when success rewarded the hunter, there was no lack of excitement. My initial experiments with a cheap folding Kodak of a vintage once commonly sold in about every drug store in the country, proved beyond any shade of doubt that the successful camera hunter had to be something of a naturalist, knowing the animals well enough to anticipate their moves and also a master stalker. A good rifle is accurate up to ranges of several hundred yards allowing a proficient shot to collect a trophy way out there, but at similar ranges my camera recorded nothing but un-recognizable specks. To get a good close-up picture meant stalking to within fifteen or twenty feet, and my early failures to get this close showed me just how little I knew about the game. It was discouraging at times, but not to the point of abandoning the idea. Something of animal psychology was being learned—not much, but still enough to show me that a whole new horizon of largely unexplored possibilities lay waiting. Failure after failure only whetted my interest and determination to master the game.

Compared to the array of equipment available today, the cameras of the time were awkward and cumbersome. The best available 35 mm models were imported from Germany and were very expensive. The variety of film available had just begun to include color and there was nothing like today's assortment of black and white film. Film speed ratings were comparatively slow and processors hated the small 35 mm format, so users of these cameras largely did their own developing and enlarging. These cameras were considered play toys of amateurs; the professionals used big cumbersome view cameras. These took beautiful pictures, but they were very heavy and awkward to operate. When one tripped the shutter on some of these they made a racket like a bucket of bolts being dumped down a dry well, and quite often a skittish subject would jump three feet in the air while the film was being exposed. The resulting photograph was a blurry reminder to the photographer that his stalking ability had far surpassed the limitations of his equipment, in no way something to cheer his soul.

Bert Riggall and most of his contemporaries carried monstrous Graflex cameras all over the mountains. He had a big telephoto lens for his 4 x 5 Graflex with fine elements encased in solid brass which weighed like a cannon. Such an outfit was a fair load for a horse, let alone a man, and was anything but foolproof with its array of film holders and other accessories, but just the same he obtained some magnificent photos with it. The large format made darkroom work much easier.

Motion picture cameras of the time were also anything but light and handy. Kodak came out with a light magazine type 16 mm camera, but these had their faults, for the fifty foot magazines were inclined to jam and the cheaply constructed pressure plates of the returnable film holders had a nasty way of relaxing with age, allowing the film to get out of focus—a very unhappy thing to discover at the end of a prolonged trip where a prize piece of footage was concerned.

The first professional-grade 16 mm motion picture cameras I saw were built like the proverbial brick outhouse—very heavy indeed—and when one used telephoto lenses there was always the problem of getting on film what you were looking at through the finder, for the finders were not of the reflex type that look through the lens, and so were subject to parallax. They had an assortment of mechanical pitfalls built into them to trip the unwary.

On occasion Bert and I guided both amateur and professional photographers using this type of equipment. Because being an adequate photographic guide meant knowing about the problems concerned, we learned something of such equipment and its use. As has been said before, a successful guide is someone very close to a jack-of-all-trades. Like the usual somewhat distorted picture of outdoor writers, we were supposed to be rugged philosophers, top riders, excellent shots, crack anglers, skillful whitewater men and outstandingly satisfactory to our women, as well as being fairly good at everything else our lives called upon us to try. Very few actually measure up to this blueprint, though the myth persists. Some of my most frustrating and astonishing experiences were with photographers.

There was the time when Franklin Crosby came out on a summer packtrip with assorted members of his numerous family, armed with a brand new Bell and Howell 16 mm motion picture camera. It was one of the first models of this rugged and very popular instrument, complete with turret head carrying three lenses. Naturally, it was spring wound, and although it carried one hundred foot rolls of film, the length of sequences was limited to about eighteen feet. Even with its shortcomings in comparison to modern equipment, this camera was about the last word in such equipment at that time.

Franklin brought about a mile of film so he and his son, George, proceeded to shoot pictures in all directions. Nothing was safe from them: people and horses alike on that trip found themselves taking part in what might be termed a cinematographic binge. Naturally action was what was wanted, but our horses proved very self-conscious about performing on film. There was always one or two snorty broncos in the outfit that would ordinarily throw a high-winding fit at the least excuse; but if the movie camera was trained on them while being packed or mounted, their resolve to come all unglued and throw things in every direction seemed to evaporate. Almost every time they walked off meek as lambs. This of course was somewhat frustrating to the photographers, nor was it the only cause for tendencies to tears.

One day George and I spotted a huge old ram lying in a pocket beside a big snowdrift at the bottom of a cliff overlooking a mountain lake, where most of the party was fishing for trout. Understandably enough George was immediately keen to stalk the ram with the camera and I volunteered to lend a hand.

There was a shallow ravine leading up the steep slope to the foot of the snowdrift, and when I looked this over with the glasses I was suddenly struck with a lightning flash of sheer genius. For this ravine had water in it which issued from the mouth of a cave in the snow—a tunnel carved by the stream and undoubtedly continuing back up to the foot of the cliff. If we crawled up this hole to its far end to the back we would likely find space enough between the snow and the rock to climb to the top edge of the drift, a position that would put us within feet of the snoozing ram.

Getting to the bottom edge of the drift was something else. But after crawling up along the water course scraping hide off our elbows and bellies on the sharp rocks, we arrived without spooking the ram. From there it was a very cool damp business making our way up through the tunnel for its roof dripped copiously on us. We were wet and shivering when we came to the foot of the cliff, but sure enough, the way was clear to climb up along a ledge to a spot close to the ram.

George went first and when he eased his eyebrows over the edge of the drift, he was within thirty feet of the sheep. With unusual calmness, he slid the camera into position and it began to whirr. Had I not been concentrating on the subject and noticed a bit more of other more important details, we might have avoided some considerable embarrassment. When the spring ran down, George carefully wound it up again and shot more film. Then the ram got restive and stood up to pose in very regal profile looking down over the country below. George rolled more film. Then the ram must have heard the camera for he looked right into George's face, his eyes widening with alarm. The next instant it was heading away on a dead run with little puffs of dust at its heels. George tracked it through his view finder like a professional.

I was just opening my mouth to cheer him for what was likely one of the best close-up pictures of a bighorn taken through the lens of a movie camera, when he began to swear. He had taken the whole series of sequences with the lens cap still in place! Naturally the film was a total blank.

Near the end of the same trip his father had an unforgettable experience to round out their initial filming adventures.

We were packing up to move and about mid-morning Bert's dog gave chase to something down in some thick stuff along the creek. Next moment a small black bear went scuttling up a tall lodgepole pine, whereupon our friend moved in for some film. Bert went down a few minutes later to find out how he was making out, and Franklin complained to him that everything was fine except that the bear wasn't moving. All it was doing was clasping the tree about forty feet from the ground looking worried—not very satisfactory for motion pictures.

"I'll move him for you," Bert volunteered and proceeded to climb the tree after the bear with the idea of making it climb higher.

But the bear did not move in the expected direction. It just hugged the tree with eyes bulging with horror as it watched Bert's progress toward it. It had apparently been in a berry patch all morning and was stuffed to the ears, for it suddenly lost all control and berries and various muck came showering down all over Bert. Upon being attacked in this unexpected fashion, Bert beat a hasty retreat, whereupon the bear came sliding down right on top of him tail first all the way. And all the way, it continued to let go loads of digested berries in a continuous shower at point blank range. When they came to the ground, the bear took off in great bounds for distant parts, while Bert took himself to the creek in an attempt to clean up. Fortunately he was wearing his hat!

Meanwhile Franklin had joined the rest of us in such uncontrolled merriment at the whole ridiculous business that he had obtained scarcely a foot of film of the episode.

The Crosby family's enthusiasm for motion pictures of wild game was afire, and although we did not realize it at the time, George's zeal carried him to considerable heights of recklessness. There was a sequel to the ram and bear episodes surpassing anything yet experienced, and although the story is a bit off-trail it deserves telling. However, I did not hear about it for a long time.

Many years later I was visiting George in his home in Minneapolis, and during the course of some reminiscing about many experiences we had shared on numerous expeditions he and various members of his family had made with us in the Rockies, he showed me various trophies. Among many other things hanging on the walls of his den there was a fragment of a canoe. It was a bit of the thwart, the V-shaped portion from the tip of the bow with a bit of broken sashcord hanging from it. When I asked George about it, he grinned and proceeded to tell me a story.

When they left us that summer when the new Bell and Howell camera was first tried out, they had taken the train east for some bass and muskie fishing at Lake of the Woods in southwestern Ontario.

One day he and his father went out to obtain some fishing pictures; Franklin with a guide in one canoe while George followed alone in another with the camera. It made a good combination to record some of the fishing sport available, and after an interesting and successful afternoon they headed back for camp.

At this time George left them to paddle back by a different route hoping to get some deer and moose pictures when these animals came out along the shore to feed in the evening. On his way across some big open water he spotted a young bull moose swimming and immediately gave chase. It was not long before he caught up, but taking pictures and paddling proved to be something of a problem for when he put down the paddle to shoot film, the moose swam quickly out of range.

But George knew something about the use of the lariat from his experience on the packtrain and there was a thirty-foot piece of braided cotton sashcord tied to the bow of the canoe. So he quickly fashioned a running noose on the loose end of it, paddled up to the moose and flipped the loop over its antlers. Then he just sat back to take pictures to his heart's content while the moose towed him across the lake.

As can happen, his enthusiasm and excitement brewed some unawareness of important things, and before he realized what was happening, the moose came close to shore where it got its feet on solid bottom. It was only when the canoe suddenly picked up speed that George took his eye from the limited field of the view finder to find his camera subject heading at a splashing run for tall timber. Before he had time to do anything about it, the canoe hit something and capsized, where-upon George found himself sitting on the bottom of the lake up to his ears in water with the camera in his lap. At this point the moose disappeared dragging the canoe at high speed.

George made his way to shore and trailed him a way. The trail was easy to follow for it was strewn with pieces of his canoe. The last sign he found was where he picked up the piece of bow thwart with a short piece of rope still attached where it had jammed under a dead-fall. This was all he had left to record the adventure for all the film was soaked with water and ruined. He proceeded to build a fire to dry out and was sitting beside it somewhat crestfallen, supperless and morose, contemplating the vagaries of wilderness cinematography, when a rescue party found him.

There are many ways to get into trouble while pursuing big game with cameras, and sometimes misadventure has a way of sneaking up on one in a most unexpected fashion.

There was the time I was guiding a professional wildlife photographer, one of the earliest and most successful of his kind. He is retired now, living a long way from the mountains where this adventure occurred, and to spare him possible embarrassment I will leave him unnamed.

He was a big, lean and powerful man well over six feet tall, good company on the trail and very keen about what he was doing; namely, putting a film together portraying packtrain life and its association with various kinds of animals. Amongst other things, he was particularly anxious to get some good close-range sequences of mountain goats in their spectacular surroundings.

Mountain goats are not an easy subject for camera work due to the country they call home, and even though they are not unduly shy or difficult to approach, the very nature of their chosen habitat offers real challenge. Anyone attempting to get within close range of a goat sooner or later almost inevitably finds himself operating his camera with his hip pockets hanging out over a thousand feet or so of eagle thoroughfare, where if a slip occurs, it will not be the fall that hurts so much as the sudden stop at the bottom. It is no kind of country for a faint heart or shaky balance, for it can be exceedingly dangerous.

The danger is graded considerably by the experience and skill of the pursuing climber, but sometimes the best of cragsmen find themselves in a tight spot. When I was much younger and full of the stuff it takes to play with goats on their choice of ground, I was convinced that a man who was a good free-climber could follow them anywhere they chose to go. But one day I was trailing three of these whiskery mountaineers across a high face, where they led me down a ledge in a fairly steep incline. It took the goats around a bulge of the mountain and when I followed it was to find myself close pressed from above by an overhang in a place where the goats had passed with ease. They were fifty yards ahead of me at a place where the ledge had been wiped out for a few feet by water and icefalls in a perpendicular chimney. Never hesitating they blithely leapt the gap and proceeded on their way.

At this point I was beginning to feel that I would be much more comfortable somewhere else, but I was committed to follow for the pack on my back and the nature of the ledge in combination with the overhang made going back extremely hazardous. I had been tolled into a natural trap. The only way out was to trail the goats. When I came to the gap in the ledge and studied it I knew very well why goats climb so much easier than a man—they have four feet to land on instead of two and those feet are specially designed to stick.

There was nothing to do but try to mimic their jump, which I proceeded to do landing on hands and feet goat fashion. I skinned myself painfully in several spots but managed to stick to the rock. Then I climbed down out of there, a much wiser man. Now when I see one of the whiskery ones looking down at me from the top of some pinnacle, I am much inclined to say, "It's your mountain, friend, and you are welcome to it."

Falling is not the only risk, for goats often double back directly over the head of the pursuing climber and have the extremely nasty habit of knocking loose rock down. Having trailed and watched them innumerable times, I am tempted to believe they do it sometimes with malice aforethought, or with a kind of grim humor difficult to share. Any way you look at it, being on the bottom end of a rock fall is no joke and can be very final. In any event, wearing a hard hat is good insurance.

But guides and hunters are not normally morbid types or negative thinkers; and on this particular occasion my photographer friend and I were not giving a thought to the possibility of trouble as we stalked two big billies feeding in a shallow dip at the top of some talus fans beneath a precipitous mountain wall about two thousand feet high.

Our stalk took us up through a strip of shintangle into a little ravine. This hid us fairly well to the base of the cliffs, where a bulge of the mountain gave concealment in a traverse toward our quarry. When we came within range my friend began to shoot film through the gate of his Eastman Special, but he had barely started when an eddy of wind gave us away. The billies instantly elevated their short tails and proceeded to climb up and away across the broken ledges of the face.

I knew that mountain like the palm of my hand and was instantly aware of a possibility, for if the goats proceeded in the direction of their retreat they might be pushed into an impossible place where they could be cornered. Ahead and above them there was a chimney with a smooth semicircular wall and an overhang at its top. If they did not cross the chimney down low enough, they would be committed to climbing into a trap. The thing to do was push them, for if goats are pressed and keep looking back, it is possible to confuse them enough to haze them into such a place where the only way out would be back past us.

I pointed out the possibility to my friend, quickly packed his camera equipment into my rucksack, shouldered the heavy tripod and led the way up over the steep rock hot on the heels of the goats. He came on strong, his eyes shining with excitement, and knowing he had considerable climbing experience I never gave him a second thought.

It was steep country but the rock was broken and rough enough to give good footing. Our Hungarian hobnails were clattering a merry tune as we scrambled in pursuit. The billies were out of sight, but pressing ahead I came within sight of them just as they were entering the chimney. Both looked back at me and obviously they were worried. Calling to my friend, I hurried, choosing a route carefully but swiftly as the billies dipped from view. Sure enough, when they came into view again, they were climbing into the blind chimney. Again I turned to urge my companion to hurry, but he was nowhere to be seen.

With a sinking feeling of dread, I backtrailed around a steep buttress wondering if he had somehow slipped and gone over the drop-off below. Then I saw him— plastered spread-eagle fashion on the face of a steep place I had just passed at a scrambling run. His complexion was almost pale green and he was hanging on with every fingernail, his knuckles white with the effort. His eyes were tight shut, and it was instantly apparent he was in the frightening throes of vertigo, a kind of nervous sickness brought on by an awareness of height that can put a climber into a paralyzing paroxysm of fear. I had seen it happen before and it is no fun for a guide and much less for the unfortunate victim.

Speaking to him quietly and reassuringly, I first found a place to safely stow my pack and the tripod. Taking a fifty-foot coil of rope out of the pack, I proceeded to help my would-be goat photographer down onto more hospitable ground.

Tying the end of the rope around him with a bowline knot, I passed the rest of the rope around a stubby little tree anchored firmly in the rock letting its free end hang down past him. Holding it to make sure he could not fall, I tried to talk him into moving, but he only groaned and hung on all the harder. So I literally pried him loose and slid him down to a ledge below, letting rope pay out as we went. He groaned some more and scraped his fingers trying to hang on, but I finally got him down to the limit of the doubled rope in spite of his best efforts to remain immovable. There was no tree for another belay at this point, but I found a projecting nubbin of rock that would do. Testing it carefully to be sure it would not crack loose, I placed my folded glove behind it to make a smooth bearing surface for the rope to slip on, and again slid the photographer down to the next available ledge, scraping all the way. He had me beat by forty pounds and was strong as a bull, which made the whole process somewhat complicated. I was sweating copiously in spite of a bitter cold breeze, when we came to rest a second time.

There another little tree gave me a third belay, and so we proceeded with me performing like a monkey on a string, prying, scrambling and cajoling. It was a tough, exasperating business, but by one means and another we finally made it to a nice wide ledge maybe two feet across within a dozen or so feet of the top of the fine talus below. There I had no more belays, which did not matter much, for my friend could fall the rest of the way without doing himself much damage, the shale being pitched at a steep angle and lying deep and loose. So I left off being the solicitous diplomat and told him very shortly to open his goddam eyes and jump. But this he refused to do, still imagining himself halfway between sky and earth.

So I resorted to other tactics. One way to shake some-one loose from vertigo is to make him or her so scorching angry that fright is forgotten. On another day I had deliberately done this when a lady climbing companion had frozen up in a tricky place. She had reacted so well, I thought for a moment she was about to pick up the nearest rock and brain me with it. Then she took off like a goat and I was hard-pressed to calm her down before she broke her neck. Then she realized why I had been so unpleasant, and we finished the climb good friends.

So without further argument I lit into the photographer calling him every kind of yellow coward; a profound dissertation well spiced with some smoky, hide-peeling adjectives learned around cow camps over my youthful years. The therapy took effect and before long he was glaring at me in an extremely warlike fashion.

I wound up by telling him, "Look, you long-eared, awkward string of misery! Either you climb down off here under your own steam or I'm going to kick you down! And if you think I'm bluffing just try me out!"

By this time he was livid with anger and with a withering look he turned his back and walked off that place as though it was fitted with stairs. A few steps down the shale slope he looked back to see me coiling my rope and preparing to climb back up the face for his cameras. Realizing what I meant to do, he came back and begged me to leave the whole outfit—worth at least three or four thousand dollars—where it lay. Nobody, he told me, was going to risk his life to get that camera; to hell with it, there was lots more where that came from! I just grinned at him and headed up the mountain. By the time I got back, he was down where we had left our horses.

He was standing with his back to me leaning against his horse and did not even glance my way as I untied halter shanks in preparation to return to camp. Then he turned with a lopsided grin and stuck out his hand in apology.

I told him to forget it, that he was not the first one that had come down with mountain sickness, nor would he be the last. He really had nothing to be ashamed about, for vertigo is a nasty thing playing no favorites. Nor was I without blame, for I should never have taken him out on that face without some preliminary climbing to condition him. I learned something that day enabling me to avoid similar trouble since.

Twenty years ago it was evident to me that the wilderness packtrain business was likely doomed in this part of the Rockies, and set about making plans for changing a way of life that had become a family tradition for over half a century. Because I have always been convinced that happiness is doing something you enjoy, it was only natural those plans led me along wilderness paths. It occurred to me that wild country and the life it contained could be profitably shown to a host of people through the mediums of photography and writing. The transition would take time and tough going, but it at least would give us a chance to make use of previous experience, an opportunity to make a living in the kind of country we all so dearly love. It was not something that had to be started cold, for some of the skill had rubbed off the photographers I had guided. For several years I had been selling stories and articles to various leading outdoor and nature magazines. Besides there had been plenty of experience talking to people across the campfires, interpreting the many adventures and things seen along the trails. So I had some considerable advantage over the rank beginner.

Apart from this, we had four boys—all about as full of steam and energy as boys can get. They had grown up close to the wilderness and had often spent time playing with sheep, goats, deer and other wild things of the mountains. The two oldest, Dick and Charlie, were big enough to be restlessly looking for new worlds to explore and like all boys they needed an outlet for their energy and imaginations. From the time they were big enough to safely handle the specially built little .22 rifle I had made up for them, they had been trained in the use of firearms, but photography was a much better outlet for their desire to hunt and would make an ideal developer for creative talent. Why not set up a wilderness photography production company in the family and let them participate? There was no end to the subject material waiting to be tapped. When I suggested we go camera hunting, they were purely delighted.

For a start, I bought them cheap, fixed-focus, box-type Kodaks. Then I arranged credit for film at the local drug store and turned them loose. Little did I realize what would transpire. At the end of a busy season I went around to pay my bill and was dumfounded at the size of it. But when I asked to see the pictures that had resulted from this unprecedented expenditure, my initial concern evaporated. There were many failures, but some were surprisingly good—sufficiently interesting and clear to warrant having some glossy enlargements made, and these were offered to a fairly high-circulation newspaper along with explanatory captions and some short columns in the nature vein. Quite a few were accepted and paid for, and ultimately appeared with full credit lines to the photographers. The editor was somewhat astonished later on to find out his new-found contributors were only ten and twelve years old.

It was not long before both boys graduated to using fine 35 mm Exakta cameras and were producing top-quality pictures.

In the meantime I had been shooting film for a lecture production through the gate of the newly acquired Bell and Howell 16 mm motion picture camera. Every spare moment was spent afield. Every spare dollar was spent on film and by the end of two years I had sufficient to splice together a film about an hour and a half long. It was a cross-sectional portrayal of about everything that walked, crawled and swam within range of my camera. If not professional, it certainly contained something of the adventures of the photographer and reflected some of the stalking skill accumulated over the years. Bighorns formed the major portion of wildlife thus illustrated because they are spectacular animals living in picturesque surroundings and have always been a fascinating source of interest to me.

They lend themselves well to such photographic study, being naturally photogenic; they live where backgrounds are rarely drab; and they respond well to human association. If one goes unarmed with an open, friendly mind among them it is not long before they accept close association; a combination of characteristics that has led me along many fascinating trails.

But looking back on that first film from the perspective of years to enable comparisons to be drawn, I now wonder how I ever had the nerve to show it in public. It lacked a great deal in technical quality, but it was, if nothing else, completely authentic. It was fairly well exposed and most of it had been shot off a tripod, but the editing was ragged. However, I held it together with a running commentary, the experience gathered from entertaining around countless campfires shared with Bert Riggall and a host of friends. Though the film had its shortcomings, it afforded the chance to try out an idea.

A friend of mine with considerable theatrical production experience looked at the film, listened to my commentary and decided that it was worth some effort. He booked up a series of eighteen shows in community halls, school auditoriums and theatres around the country, and I was committed to sink or swim.

The opening show was in a large hall in the city of Lethbridge, where the boys accompanied me to participate in the festivities, as they had shot some of the film. It had been preceded by much promotional fanfare over radio and in the newspapers. I had butterflies fluttering under my ribs as zero hour approached; but when the doors opened and people flooded in to jam the place till it could hold no more, I knew that heady feeling known only to stage performers stepping out in front of the footlights and looking out over a packed house on a sell-out opening night. The butterflies were still giving some trouble, as I warmed up with a short explanatory introduction prior to dimming the lights and turning on the projector. But then the big rams began to parade across the screen and something about them lent confidence. I forgot about everything except taking the crowd on a guided tour through the mountains—exactly what I had been doing for years —only this depended more on my ability to make the scenes on the screen come alive, giving the audience a feeling of participation rather than just being viewers. The whole performance went so smoothly I surprised myself. The applause that followed was gratifying, for it was much more than just polite and indicated real enjoyment.

Thanks to my friend, Harry Baalim, who was promoting the show, the whole tour was a resounding success. We had a show in a different town six nights a week for three weeks, and by the end of it I felt like I had walked on short rations from one end of the Rockies to the other. Show business proved to be hard work, but it was interesting and gratifying.

That began a branch of my life I have enjoyed ever

since. The following winter my trail led me east to
Detroit and New York through various bookings at private clubs, sportsmen's meetings and some new adventures. In Detroit I met Jack Van Coevering, the famous
outdoor columnist with the Detroit *Free Press*, who invited me to appear on his television show. This medium
of entertainment and communication was then very new,
and I had the unique experience of seeing myself on the
monitoring screen before I had ever watched a show on a
regular television set. Then came an opportunity to make
a first appearance in the professional circuits.

Some friends in Minneapolis arranged to have me
make an audition to appear on a scheduled series under
the auspices of the Minnesota Natural History Society,
where they invite speakers and filmmakers from around
the world to participate in an annual program held every
winter. I appeared before a board of directors to show
them my film with some secret misgivings. To this day I
am somewhat at loss to know why they confirmed the
booking, but approve it they did.

In due course I came to the Hall of Arts to put on two
shows in one evening, for the series was so popular, the
building would not accommodate the crowd in one session.
My introduction was given by the president of the association, Dr. Clayton Rudd, and it was the shortest, most
pointed one I ever experienced. He stepped forth on the
huge lighted platform ahead of me and said, "Ladies and
gentlemen, I take pleasure in introducing the only man I
ever met with nerve enough to bring the first film he ever
made to a place like this! I give you Andy Russell!"

I found myself standing out there in a spotlight in
that vast platform big enough to corral forty horses with
room to spare wondering how anyone could be so reck-

less. The footlights were shining up in my face and I was largely blinded by the spotlight coming down from some place high above. Dimly I could see the place was packed and right then I would have cheerfully faced a charging grizzly by way of a trade. The welcoming applause did little to still the butterflies. A bit to one side out of the corner of my eye I could see an enormous screen and had a horrifying thought that my little 16 mm film would fade out to nothing on its vast expanse. A microphone reared its head like a cobra ready to strike in front of my nose. Right then I came about as close to complete paralysis as I have ever been. But then remembering there were people out there in the audience I had known and entertained in a different way for many years, I knew it was impossible to let them down. So I lit an imaginary campfire out among the footlights, dreamed up a mountain lifting its craggy head against the stars out back, forgot where I was and began to talk.

When the old rams came walking beautifully out onto the screen with the sun reflected in their golden eyes, as usual they were an instant hit, and a spontaneous little ripple of applause drifted out across the theatre. Then everything came easier, and before I realized time was passing, the show came to an end. After a fifteen minute interval I was back for the second session and once more the people loved it. Following almost four continuous hours, I knew what it was to be completely wrung out, utterly exhausted and at the end of my rope. Surrounded by smiling friends, many of them dressed in evening clothes that were a vast contrast to my western garb and boots, I felt like an adventurer who had taken a big chance and somehow survived.

I was staying with people I knew and we were all invited to the house of one of their friends for refreshments. Our hostess was a middle-aged lady of Irish extraction, outspoken and warmhearted. When she asked what I needed most, a drink or something to eat, I suddenly realized I was ravenous. When I told her I was hungry, she disappeared and in no time came back with a big plate heaped with steaming corned beef and cabbage. How she prepared it so quickly in the middle of the night, I will never know, but never did anything taste so good. Sitting there in her richly appointed house, I polished off that delicious repast with all the enthusiasm of a starving Indian. I do not recall the lady's name, but I will never forget her, for apart from being very attractive, her hospitality was wonderful—something enjoyed and remembered by a mountain man a long way from home.

My photographic work with the bighorns and associated species carried me into many places near and far among thousands of people, and in due course of subsequent events I received an invitation to make a film record of bighorns from birth to death for the historical archives of a wealthy foundation. It was an exciting prospect, even if I had some reservations about accepting it, for the people I was working with knew nothing of the problems involved in such an ambitious undertaking. Too often when you deal with big organizations, creative work gets paralyzed and buried in a jungle of office politics where there is no feeling for, or understanding of, the problems confronting the person responsible for putting the picture together so it can be enjoyed and understood.

But the challenge was irresistible and the problems involved in producing such a film could be surmounted. Had I not been aware of this, I would not have been invited to discuss its various points in the first place, so I signed the contract, and with Dick and Charlie to help me, prepared to launch what turned out to be one of the most interesting and at the same time extremely frustrating efforts of our entire experience.

11

Beginning the Long Hunt

Napoleon once said, "The man who knows where he is going, when he begins, will never go far." When we headed out in early August of 1957 with our gear loaded on a string of ten horses for the heart of the bighorn mountains adjacent to our ranch near Waterton Lakes National Park, we certainly did not know where our trails would lead us or what the next couple of years had in store. This was likely a very good thing. We thought our problems would be mainly concerned with the wild sheep, but it was not to be that way, and if we had initially known the troubles we would encounter, we may have been tempted to call the whole idea a waste of time and effort. This would have been too bad, for as things turned out some grand experience would have been missed.

There was a certain aura of sadness going with us up the trail while the music of Swiss bells on the horses rang in our ears punctuating the anticipation of spending the rest of the summer rambling among the familiar peaks.

For that summer my old friend and companion of count-less days spent among the Rockies had left us. I was aware of a void in my life no one else could ever fill. Dick and Charlie would also miss their grandfather very much for they had always been close to him; a kind of wonderfully warm relationship between boys and a grandparent I had once known and enjoyed with mine.

Certainly if Bert Riggall could have known what we were planning to do—what we were attempting on this tremendous hunt with our cameras—he would have smiled and approved; for he truly loved the bighorns and had always been fascinated by them. He had known them so well, he could often foretell what they would do hours before they did it. As I have often said, he knew what the ewe said to her lamb. Working with him had been my keystone to my own knowledge of these grand animals, the real foundation of experience fostering this plan to record their lives on film.

We pitched our first camp on the mountain meadow overlooking the highest of Twin Lakes under the 2500-foot face of the Continental Divide marking the border between Alberta and British Columbia. The mountain flowers were in their full extravaganza of bloom here at timberline, the grass lush and deep and the timber full of bird song. We were outfitted with good equipment and thousands of feet of color film for our pair of Bell and Howell 16 mm motion picture cameras, improved versions of the same kind George Crosby and I had used on our epic stalk of the ram at the top of the snow tunnel in this same place. We also had still cameras with us for record-ing various things of interest for our photo files.

We not only planned to film the characteristics and habits of the bighorns but also of associated species; for to portray a true cross section of any animal's life including man, it is very necessary to capture something of the various kinds of associated life. For always there are various links, direct and indirect, illustrating interdependence of food chains and various environmental features keying the whole vast and intricate tapestry pattern of life forms together.

Over years of rambling and observing the life of the Rockies, one's awareness of a kind of vast and beautiful interwoven design becomes sharp and positive. We humans are not separate from the life in these mountains, but part of it, and by the very weight of our intelligence and dominance placed in a position of trust bound to recognition of responsibility. If we could manage to illustrate this in subtle yet forcefully clear fashion, I was very sure the value of the resulting film would be vastly enhanced.

So began our hunt. From the first morning we stepped out of the tent door to look out across the sloping meadow down through a gap in the spruces to the dancing blue waters of the lake, every day held promise of many different and exciting things to record.

Almost immediately we began to see sheep. Five rams were feeding on the shelves above the talus fans beyond the lake that first morning, but their position was impossible to approach due to the almost perpendicular nature of the face; so we left them undisturbed and headed out along a trail leading over a low pass to the south in search of more.

In the high hanging basin beyond the pass three more rams were feeding. While we climbed toward them, the first five we had spotted from camp came around the mountain shoulder to join them. This was a typical bachelor's club summering up here along the backbone of the continent. Behind them we could stand on a ridge top looking both ways down drainages ultimately ending in Hudson Bay and the Pacific Ocean.

We stalked them using much different techniques than once employed, for instead of sneaking up ravines and gumshoeing through patches of scrub, we made our approach in the open without trying to hide. Going slow and letting the rams see us all the way, we finally reached a tiny bench on the talus slope among some old caved-in grizzly diggings where a silvertip had once excavated for ground squirrels. There we were within camera range.

The rams fed up at the top of the talus under the cliffs fifty yards above us. As they moved we slowly trailed along behind them. While we were shooting them, two goats wandered out on the face a thousand feet or more above us and triggered a small rock fall. It was of no great volume but directly overhead, noisy and spectacular with clouds of dust as plate-sized chunks of rock came leaping down at us. Our photography came to a sudden end, for in leaping about in the process of dodging this unexpected barrage we gave the rams the jitters and they climbed up on some ledges a hundred feet up the cliffs to stand gazing down curiously at us as though trying to figure out what kind of game this was. It was too late by this time to pursue them further, for the sun was far enough west to put their location in shade, so we headed back to camp.

The following morning we were back to find the rams feeding in the same general location, and as we climbed to their level the whole bunch fed up to the foot of a snow-drift at the base of the cliffs. Three big rams suddenly broke into frolic on the snow, leaping and swapping ends, playfully butting each other, evidently in such good spirits they just had to blow off some steam. Dick and I alternated with our cameras in capturing a record of this lighthearted activity, before the whole bunch again climbed onto the shelves overhead.

This time we climbed after them, Dick and I with tripods and cameras balanced on our shoulders, while Charlie carried extra lenses and film. They gave us some dramatic shots in excellent light before clouds rolled in from the west, forcing us to quit. Unlike rifle hunting, successfully stalking game with cameras depends entirely on having adequate light, a condition of the game often taxing one's patience.

Next morning we woke to find the mountains enveloped in thick mist with a cold wind blowing in from the northeast. Saddling my horse I headed back to the ranch to take care of some correspondence, read the mail and send some film for processing. Returning to camp in late afternoon I found Dick and Charlie beside themselves with excitement.

About noon the fog had lifted and the sun came out between fluffy rags of clouds clinging to the peaks, so the boys went fishing; Dick taking his fly rod around to the far shore of the lake by camp while Charlie went to the lower one about a quarter of a mile south. He had been fishing about an hour when he heard a queer whistling sound high on the mountain directly across the lake, and looked up just in time to see a great slab of rock slowly tip off the cliff face near the top of the peak like a great stone door falling from its hinges. As it fell it gathered speed with a rising crescendo of sound developing into a thunderous roar as it hit the solid front of the mountain below shattering itself into thousands of pieces. Instantly the whole slope opposite him was a leaping mass of boulders enveloped in billowing clouds of dust, the thunder of it filling the mountains with echoes. Some of the larger boulders came down almost to the lake and a few went into it with great splashes. Luckily for Charlie he had the whole lake between him and the rockfall, or he might have been badly injured or killed.

Dick was nowhere near, but he saw the fall and knew Charlie was somewhere near it. Scared and worried he came over the ridge between the lakes as fast as his feet could carry him. By the time he arrived most of the rockfall had come to rest, and he found his brother safe and sound, though somewhat wide-eyed and breathless at the spectacle he had witnessed at such close range. The air was thick with dust, which had largely settled in a fine film over everything by the time I arrived in camp. Rocks were still falling sporadically and continued to do so to varying degrees all night.

After breakfast in the morning we set out to inspect the trail and found considerable rock still coming down which made any kind of trail-clearing operation hazardous, so I climbed up to one side under a sheltering overhang to film something I had never seen before: a talus fan being actually built before my eyes. Sometimes the air was full of a shower of loose stuff coming down a shallow gully from fifteen hundred feet. Some of it came directly over me, but the overhanging ledge deflected it and I paid it little attention. But my feeling of safety proved to be a bit premature.

After I had been there for nearly half an hour, somewhere above a slab of rock about six inches through and shaped like a wagon wheel cut loose and rolled up onto its edge. This gave it much greater velocity as it spun and leapt down the gully and suddenly it bounded out of it on the far side in great leaps taking it sometimes more than a hundred feet at a jump. A bit above my level it struck something that caused it to glance and turn so that it re-crossed the gully in a huge bound sending it whistling past my ear so close I felt the wind off it. My interest in further rockslide photography began to wane rapidly at that point, and I took myself elsewhere.

Many times over the years I have seen evidence of rockfalls, sometimes even hearing big ones come down in the distance. Small occurrences of this nature are com-monplace but this was the first time any of us had ob-served a fairly big one at close range. This fall continued sporadically for three days and left a light-colored yel-lowish scar down the face of the mountain that was clearly visible for years afterward.

The weeks went by as we wandered the mountains with our packtrain, moving camp along a route that took us across the park from north to south until we reached a magnificent area overlooking Boundary Creek and the mountains inside Glacier Park, Montana. From the cook tent door we were facing south toward an array of peaks glittering with snow and ice with great cliffs dropping towards green and blue water, where lakes lay pocketed at timberline. This was prime mountain goat country but no sheep ever go into it. But by simply turning around and looking up the talus slopes back of the tents we could see bighorns—ewes, lambs and rams, gamboling, feeding, and traveling the heavy trails cut into the loose shale. There were goats here too as well as the occasional grizzly and many mule deer.

The big-eared muleys, one of the most graceful animals in all the mountains, fed and wandered past our camp every day. It was not uncommon to see the big bucks feeding on the same hanging meadows and talus fans with the sheep.

We found where one big buck had tried to cross a strip of hard old ice where a big snowdrift had melted away exposing a leftover from previous years. Having likely used this trail when the snow was soft to cross a high slope under Carthew Peak, the buck may have been careless. Whatever the reason, he slipped and plummeted over a thousand feet to his death among jagged rocks below. Just previous to our discovery, a wolverine had found the carcass and was feeding on it. But in late afternoon the place was in deep shade, so we left without trying to film it.

When we returned the following morning, a grizzly had located the dead buck, fed on it and buried the remains under a mound of loose rock and dirt. We were sitting on a shelf on the face of the cliff about a hundred yards from the cache suspecting the grizzly was lying asleep in a patch of shintangle scrub not far away. As we watched, Dick spotted the wolverine coming down off the front of a mountain directly across the big basin beyond about a mile away. Traveling as though led by a string in a straight line oblivious to contours, the wolverine never paused till it arrived at the buried deer. There it sniffed around very nervously inspecting the grizzly's cache, obviously wanting no part of being confronted by the big bear. Finally, between worried looks in all directions, the wolverine began digging furiously to uncover a portion of the deer's hindquarters. Upon baring a part of the haunch, it quickly tore off a piece of meat and went galloping away to disappear into a gully beyond where a small stream coursed down between patches of green herbage.

Seizing the opportunity to get some rare footage, I slung a camera and tripod over my shoulder and ran down a narrow inclining ledge to the top of a shale slope above and a bit behind where the wolverine had disappeared in hopes of filming the animal when it came out on the far side of the gully. But it did not show up. I was standing over the camera with my eye to the viewfinder when it suddenly came running right past me heading back to the deer. There it quickly tore off another piece of meat and came galloping back to the gully, where it disappeared between two rows of monkey flowers and water willow herb flanking the little stream. I had filmed it going and coming and was beside myself to get a shot of it now, for by moving a little I could see it was scrubbing the dirt off the meat in the water prior to eating it, something nobody had ever recorded or even hinted at in respect to wolverine habit. But before I could slip into position giving me a clear shot, an eddy of wind gave my scent to the wolverine and it immediately galloped away down slope to vanish in a strip of timber.

It was a fascinating adventure with nature's biggest member of the weasel clan, an animal that has more myth and sheer prevarication attached to it than perhaps any other. It has been credited with being so utterly ferocious that even bears give it the trail, which is utter nonsense, for a grizzly or a black bear could flatten the biggest wolverine with a casual blow of its paw. However, the wolverine is a very strong and intelligent animal, and a predator of wild sheep when conditions are in its favor. Charles Sheldon reported observing various instances where wolverines had attacked and killed Dall sheep in the Mount McKinley region of Alaska. We found evidence of wolverines preying on sheep in the Yukon and

Mule deer are one of nature's most perfect creations

Packtrain on the move, following bighorn sheep in the mountains of Alberta

Caribou and Dall sheep share the northern ranges

Traveling by dog team on the ice of Kluane Lake, Yukon Territory, in spring

ABOVE: *A bull caribou on the flats not far from the old site of Charles Sheldon's winter cabin in Alaska*

A herd of caribou bulls skylined in Alaska

RIGHT: *A hunting camp where all we had to look after was us*

BELOW: *Kay catching our supper out of a wild river*

BOTTOM: *Fat venison for the winter that we stalked across a rockslide in stocking feet*

*Our trails rambled through
magnificent country in summer*

*Typical resting position of a bighorn bachelors' club—
not an angle of the compass they are not watching*

Dall ram on Sheldon's Mountain

Skull and skeleton mark the end of another old, broken-horned veteran

Broken-horn ram photographed by Bert Riggall in 1934; the horn was shattered in a fight

*Packtrain travel in the old days, in a trackless section
of the Rockies of British Columbia*

*The skull and horns of a classic stone ram
taken in northern British Columbia*

have also noted instances where these animals have killed bighorns as far south as the 49th parallel. So this particular opportunity to obtain rare footage of a wolverine feeding on the carcass of a buck was pertinent to a production dealing with the habitat of wild sheep, being aptly illustrative of a joining link in the life pattern of these mountains.

Another animal we often observed in the vicinity of bighorns, on occasion feeding almost under their feet, was the tiny pika, sometimes called the rock rabbit. These energetic little animals live in the coarse rockslides of old glacial moraines above timberline and spend the last half of summer and early fall busily collecting forage, which they deposit in neat little haystacks under overhangs sheltered from rain and exposed to the sun. There the hay piles cure in the sun and drying wind for use in winter when the pikas run about among the loose rock under feet of snow. While stalking and filming sheep we were almost always within earshot of the bleating calls of these little animals. There was a colony of them, along with several hoary marmots, over the ridge from camp amongst a great pile of boulders.

The marmots were easy to film, but the pikas posed a problem, for they are very quick, erratic and unpredictable in their movements. One would be sitting on a rock staring into my face from a range of a few feet, fairly vibrating with its alarm call, and the next instant before I could blink an eye the same animal would be almost between the legs of my tripod busily collecting ground herbage for its private cache. Too much of the film I exposed trying to film these small creatures showed a beautiful place in sharp detail where a pika had recently been. All this contributed to a considerable waste of film while trying to put together a comprehensive sequence of this little competitor in wild sheep range.

One amusing incident was observed while working with the pikas at the foot of a steep scree under some shelves and cliffs. A very industrious and hard-working pika was gathering plants right in front of me among the boulders. It would fill its face to the point of wearing a green mustache half as big as itself, then go scooting off up the slope about a hundred fifty feet to its private haystack. There the load would be arranged on the heap and it would return for more. While it was gone another pika from about the same distance farther up the mountain would come down and help itself to the hay, and thus my nearest neighbor's pile was getting no bigger in spite of its best efforts. This went on for some time, until the thief slipped up on his timing and met the unaware donator of hay face to face at the haystack.

There was a sudden agitated flurry of pika profanity and much chasing, nipping and squeaking through, around and over rocks until the enterprising resident from up the mountain was driven with much gusto back into its own territory. The problem thus solved to its satisfaction, the first pika came back to gather more hay, the incident forgotten.

This was the only time when I ever observed private hay piles being robbed by other pikas. Occasionally, when a very choice and limited location is involved with no others within reach, pikas will store their feed in a sort of communal storage ground. I once saw one such haystack in the Yukon which must have contained close to fifty or sixty pounds of feed being attended by a number of pikas. They appeared to be getting along well and had apparently come to some kind of understanding.

While my friend, Fred Mannix, and I were standing and watching the activity of this place, a beautiful weasel appeared on the scene, and immediately every pika was up on the top of a convenient boulder bleating in consternation. Weasels and pine martins are the deadly enemies of pikas and apparently the little haymakers figured their chances of survival were better if they stayed above ground.

Regardless of the source of interest, the many facets of life in wild sheep ranges are almost limitless in variety, offering unending opportunity to the naturalist-cinematographer to record pictures illustrating the association between species. When we started out on any morning we never knew what the day held in store, and sometimes our plans were completely changed by sudden opportunities to collect and record action and life appearing unexpectedly before us. Hence the use of a shooting script in this kind of photography can only be utilized in the broadest fashion, for in reality the animals themselves are the script writers and there is no way to foretell what they will deliver next.

As always we were plagued by weather to a certain extent, sometimes held back by poor light conditions to obtain a film record of things we saw and sorely wanted. But then, to compensate for those times when everything appeared to be conspiring against us, we experienced those wonderful golden days when real nuggets of material were observed and recorded. On such occasions we tended to forget the hours of fruitless work and the prospective story literally seemed to blossom before our eyes. It was the kind of work that could never be boring; the unknown quantities and the challenges were always there to beckon us on. We were something like prospectors looking for the mythical pot of gold at the end of the rainbow; we were sure it was there somewhere, but there was no telling what form it would take. The answer to the secret lay around the next bend of the trail or over the next ridge.

12

Winter Sheep Trails

Winter came early that year, preceded by a cold wet fall that made successful camera hunting very difficult. Weeks went by when rain, wind and snow squalls drove down off the Continental Divide in a seemingly unending procession of turbulent, cold storms that kept us off the high slopes. It was not till late November, when hours of color film sunshine had narrowed down to four or five a day under the best conditions, that I was able to spend any really successful time with the bighorns. Even when the sun was shining brightly the wind chill up above timberline was something to be reckoned with, and even with winterized cameras it was often wasteful of film to attempt photography. More than once when the camera ground to a halt, I opened it to find the film broken and the film chamber jammed with footage all crinkled and folded, completely useless. Film breaks easily when it is cold, a conditional hazard about as frustrating and trying to the patience as anything can be. Working barehanded to clear such a mess was not pleasant; but part of the problem was solved when a friend gave me a pair of old-time, pure silk glove liners—the kind stagecoach drivers wore under buckskin gloves to handle the reins of four- and six-horse teams. They were museum pieces, but with these in the camera case for such emergencies, the business of changing lens and film became much less of an endurance contest with the elements.

Meanwhile, Dick and Charlie were back in school except for weekends, so most of the time I worked alone. The sheep were on their wintering grounds much lower and closer to the ranch than they were in summer, enabling me to work with them without undergoing the rigors of winter camping.

One of the things I was particularly anxious to record was a battle between two big rams during the contests of the rutting season, consequently as much time as weather allowed was spent aloft above timberline. It was a hectic and often risky pursuit, for apart from the wind, a real menace at times as has been accounted, the trails and ledges were often icy and dangerous. A chinook or a period of warm sun melts the snow, and the water oozing out over the bare rock of exposed ledges freezes in a thin layer of clear ice. When a light skiff of snow covers such places it makes a trap set to catch the unwary climber. Short of wearing crampons on one's boots, which are almost impossible to use on any other kind of footing, there is no kind of footgear that will hold on this stuff. So the only alternative was to exercise extreme caution and go slowly when one was not sure of the footing. On short winter days this hinders the photographer, a combination that often kept shooting time down to a frustrating success level. It is this kind of thing that develops a brand of patience akin to that credited to Job, and never was this quality of character more necessary.

Several times during November and December I was within sight and sound of big rams tangling in head-battering collisions at a distance, but was unable to get within range in time to record it.

Sometimes I came close. A big ram with heavy, full curl horns was escorting a small bunch of ewes on the side of a rock outcrop along the flank of a high open ridge across a canyon perhaps a quarter of a mile from my position. While I was glassing them, another big ram showed up coming down along the ridge from above, and then a third one appeared climbing from a scrub-covered slope below. Both of these potential competitors of the first ram's harem were burly big herdmasters and just as obviously both seemed to know exactly where they were going. When they came together I wanted to be close. My best approach was straight across the canyon but this meant dropping down through a thick strip of timber into the rocky gulch below before I could reach the bare, wind-whipped side with the sheep.

It was worth a try, although the north slope was deep in snow—a place where the sun never shone in winter, sheltered by the mountain from the wind. Slinging my camera pack over my shoulders I headed down the slope on the run and made good time till I hit the timber where the snow was well over my knees. In the gulch I bogged down in snow up to my armpits. While I was fighting to extricate myself, the three rams came together and knowing there was no time left to get into position, I just subsided and watched.

The boss ram had his ewes bunched on a pinnacle, a fine place for defense, and was standing on a small ledge below them watching his rivals. Both of them were obviously feeling belligerent and in the mood for trouble. After some preliminary skirmishing and displaying of horns, they collided in mid-air, horn to horn with a crash that rang off the slopes and jolted them to their heels. For a moment or two after the collision, both rams stood as though dazed looking off into the distance, which condition is not surprising for the jolt of their mighty horns is terrific. Then they backed away, squared off and came together again.

Meanwhile the first ram was just standing a few yards above them looking on. When they began getting set for a third smash he moved fast to intercept them. With amazing timing he launched himself down the steep slope and met both simultaneously from the side just as they came together. The result was catastrophic for his rivals, for he knocked both of them down and ended the fight right there. Number three ram that had come from below lost all interest in the proceedings and turned back down the mountain from where he had come. Number two ram also turned away and he appeared to be hurt, for through the glasses his mouth was hanging open although there was no evidence of blood. The victorious old herdmaster stood watching them leave, his magnificent horns held proudly showing in silhouette against a snowdrift, and then he turned back to rejoin the ewes.

It was one of those unforgettably dramatic things a cameraman sometimes gets the chance to observe with no opportunity to record it. One can only hope that by staying with his camera subjects, he can someday take advantage of the law of averages and be within range when nature contrives to lift the curtain on a similar scene. Such reflections, however, were small comfort; I was feeling quite low in my mind, for no one knows better that no two scenes are never quite the same. This was a rare incident which I would likely never have the opportunity to observe again.

Sometimes my pursuit of rutting sheep had its amusing sidelights, even if those first attempts to film a fight were seemingly jinxed. One fine weekend morning Dick and Charlie were working with sheep some distance away across a narrow side canyon to Pass Creek Valley; Dick was close to five ewes with a fine ram, while Charlie was stalking another small bunch about a thousand feet farther up the mountain. Dick's bunch led him up a steep chimney over a rocky spur, and while he was climbing at their heels another ram appeared out of a jumble of broken ledges below to fall in line behind him. Dick was at first unaware of him, but then must have heard him, for he looked back from a precarious position in the middle of the almost perpendicular chimney to find a pair of heavy, efficient-looking horns only a jump or two behind his hip pockets. Judging from the speed with which he made the rest of the distance to the top, the idea of those horns so close to his exposed posterior bothered him. He popped out on the lip of the rim so suddenly, his original models spooked and scattered like chaff in the wind.

The rut of the wild sheep offers much action to be filmed, but in spite of continuous trying whenever weather allowed, I did not get a chance to record a fight that winter. But there were other facets of the mating moon that were collected.

Naturally, the ewes come in for much vigorous attention, sometimes to the point of exhaustion, especially where the proportion of males is high. For when a ewe comes into oestrus in the vicinity of a group of rams, she is often pursued and covered by several rams in succession. More than once I have seen ewes literally driven to submission over extremely rough terrain at a dead run where footing even for mountain sheep was so bad, one had cause to wonder how they escaped severe injury or death. Sometimes after intercourse with several males, a ewe would lie down in her tracks exhausted, only to be approached by a ram, struck sharply with a forefoot, brought to her feet and covered yet again.

Association between rams at this time is not all competitive and warlike, for more than once a big old ram, his nose bent in permanent misalignment from many fights, was observed traveling with a younger and more nimble four or five year old, which was tolerated and allowed to stay close even when a ewe was being attended. Perhaps this kind of association is a holdover from the period of comradeship during the indolent summer, the tolerant association of the bachelor's clubs. Perhaps it is a kind of cooperation of even less explainable portent where the dominance of one is recognized and accepted by the other, the attitude of the smaller male being a certain willingness to adopt the subordinate role in return for opportunities to enjoy some opportunities. Such a tolerance is never displayed between two old rams. Always it is between a fully mature male and a much younger one, the latter being subservient to every dominant move the bigger one makes. Just the same, when a ewe comes into heat causing very violent competition between big males, the younger ram will serve her while the old ones strive to addle each other's brains. And strangely enough, even while the young ram is engrossed in copulation and completely vulnerable, the older partner will sometimes tolerate the action. It is a strangely permissive association between a king ram and his lesser prince consort in which the stripling seems to get a surprisingly large portion of the fruits of the game.

On the other side of the ledger, I have seen a young intruder that insisted on hanging around too close to an older ram treated deliberately as if he were a female. No matter if he accepted the dominance of the bigger ram without showing any inclination to fight, he would be shouldered, sometimes struck with a front foot and if he still stayed too close, mounted in a kind of mock copulation.

Always in any herd where several males are present, there is a kind of pecking order established where their loose-knit association has been long enough to form an order of dominance. This is punctuated by displaying of horns and much strutting of physical attributes fascinating to watch. Hence, while there is considerable chasing and parading, the actual breeding activity is carried out with relatively little actual combat; head-to-head battering is by no means something occurring every day. When it does happen, it can be violent. Very often the tough horns are splintered and broken. Where the bridges of their noses come into contact they are often broken—not just once but perhaps many times over several seasons until the ram's profile becomes almost grotesque. Quite often, as late as May following the rut, rams have been observed with pus running from an open wound over a broken nose bone. Occasionally a ram will slip and injure a knee on the rocks during a fight, sometimes severely enough to be permanently lamed. When secondary pushing and shouldering takes place, the rams often strike at each other and sometimes a hoof connects with the heavy, prominent testicles. Just how injurious this can be is something of a question, though it takes the fight out of the unfortunate one at the time.

Several times I have seen rams with abscessed scrotums in late winter and early spring, but I suspect this is caused by freezing. Such freezing occurs among domestic bulls on occasion, and when it does, it renders the animal sterile; so if the condition happens among rams under certain circumstances, they too are likely sterile as a result.

Winter hunting with cameras, though often cruel in the cold and the wind, has the same qualities of expectation, challenge, beauty and interesting sidelights found in summer; it is an endless source of interest to the naturalist.

We never encountered goats on the wintering grounds of the sheep here on the drainage of the Waterton River, for these whiskery cragmasters choose much more inhospitable country. On some of the stone sheep ranges of northern British Columbia these two species share the same mountains although it is usually on different levels.

We often saw elk and mule deer mingling with wintering bighorns; competing for the same feed, and using the same general shelter during bad storms. Although the mule deer are predominantly browsers, therefore adding little by weight of competition for feed in their association with the sheep, the elk are something to be reckoned with on the limited range of winter. Being big and gregarious animals with appetites comparable to their size, they browse and graze and are a definite limiting factor on sheep and deer populations where they occupy the same range.

Elk are excellent climbers negotiating the high frozen

slopes used by sheep with amazing sureness of foot. But their size added to unusual weather conditions can sometimes get them into trouble.

The previous winter after a stretch of weather with a good deal less snow than usual, the temperature dropped in mid-January to twenty below zero and stayed there for about ten days. Then about dusk one evening, the northeast wind suddenly switched to the southwest, a balmy chinook shooting the temperature up sixty degrees in a couple of hours. To make it even more of a contrast it began to rain, and when morning came we found ourselves looking out over what was likely the biggest skating rink in the world. With little snow over it, the ground was iron hard and still way below zero when the rain hit it. Where ground cover was sparse or on the face of naked rock everything was covered with a clear sheet of hard ice an inch or more thick.

Some of my horses were caught in a little valley on the north side of the ranch and were just standing in their tracks, afraid to move. To ride a horse was utterly impossible, so I undertook to move them onto better ground afoot. It took me almost three hours to move them a mile onto another piece of pasture deep in grass where there was little ice. In the course of events several of them took hard falls and I also found myself in mid-air more than once, observing my boots going skyward past my nose at high speed and coming down with a jar that shook every bone in my frame. Apart from my difficulties in staying on my feet, the whole procedure was about as unique as anything ever attempted with horses.

Temperatures dropped back to normal again, so the ice covering the country was slow to go. One morning my big German shorthair pointer, Seppi, jumped a snow-

shoe hare on an open slope near our house and the resulting pursuit was a comedy. The snowshoe was confused by being caught in the open and ordinarily would
have been caught, but every time the dog got within
reach, the hare dodged, whereupon poor Seppi would go
tail over teakettle trying to turn. He was completely beside himself as he scrambled, cartwheeled, bayed and
cried. The demoralized hare finally made his way back to
cover and escaped. Seppi came to my call giving me a
very disgusted look, for like all dogs he hated to be
laughed at and there was no way I could restrain myself.

Up in sheep country it was about impossible for a
man carrying a pack to travel without special gear, and
even when this getting from one spot to another was so
slow it was uselessly unproductive. There was plenty of
feed for the game up on the windswept ridges and
shoulders, but in between every gully and draw was an
unbroken sheet of ice covering everything. A pine squirrel
would have trouble keeping its feet on the steep slopes,
so I contented myself watching the game from the flats.

One Friday after school Dick and Charlie took off on
a hike along the foot of the mountains toward Indian
Springs and came back to report forty-two bull elk out
on the prairie flats half a mile from the rocks.

This would make a spectacular shot with the movie
camera, so next morning we were out early. During the
night the elk had moved and when we found them the
bunch had split and were in an impossible place to make
a stalk. So we decided to try a drive, something we rarely
attempted for it generally ends up in a fiasco. While the
boys made a big circle to come back on the bulls from the
south, I hid myself in a gully with the idea of filming
them as they passed between me and the mountain.

For half an hour nothing happened. I stood behind the camera on top of its tripod admiring a fine morning under a cloudless sky with no wind at my level, although the peaks in all directions were adorned with banners of flying snow streaming away on a southwest wind. It was crisp but not uncomfortably cold. About the time I decided Dick and Charlie had lost the bulls, I spotted some cow elk standing looking my way on the edge of a timbered bench about a mile to the north. Then they came traveling diagonally down the slope at a trot with more cows, calves and young bulls pouring out of the trees behind them.

To my astonishment they came directly across country toward me in a line that would cross the gully right in front of me in exactly the opposite direction of the expected bulls. I counted three hundred twenty-seven head of them as they poured down across a long gentle slope in a long line. They showed no sign of being aware of me, but when they came to the gully only a part of the herd crossed it, the whole bunch coming to a stop with some beginning to feed and the rest just standing as though enjoying the sun. After shooting a roll of film, I just stood watching this scene of teeming life waiting for more action, but never dreaming the direction it would take.

The big old lead cow of the bunch began working her way up along a big game trail into the rocky gully leading straight up the mountain; a trail they often used in summer and fall but right now looking impossible for anything but bighorns. As she went, the whole herd began to follow slowly and methodically picking their way up onto the steep, icy country. Occasionally one would slip a bit, but none fell, and so they went until the trail up the gully was a solid line of elk. But the going was getting rougher and most of the herd gave it up to turn and pick their way back down swinging back north toward the bench where they had started.

But fifty head, with the old cow in the lead, kept going. Higher and higher they climbed, up into the broken ledges where the mountain face was more than forty-five degrees in pitch and the gulch was flanked on both sides by cliffs like giant steps. There the cow turned sharp to the north out along a horizontal ledge, a continuation of the same trail.

They were now a thousand feet above me and committed to the mountain, for this trail was too narrow for them to turn around. To attempt it on this footing would mean a fall to sure death over the cliffs below. Realizing the potential of this trap they had got themselves into, I grabbed the camera and climbed swiftly up to a point just under the rock directly across the gully under them.

The elk were picking their way carefully traversing the ledge out toward an open windswept shoulder. There they came to where their trail crossed a gully about a dozen feet wide, sloped steeply and floored with ice and dropping off below them almost perpendicularly toward the top of a narrow talus fan directly opposite me. There the lead cow stopped bringing the whole line behind her to a standstill. From where I looked on incredulously through my glasses, it appeared that the whole bunch was trapped, doomed to stay where they were until they starved or fell to their death.

For a few minutes not an animal moved. But then a young cow midway along the line got restive and tried to turn around. She almost made it, but her hind feet slipped, throwing her off balance and she came over backwards off the edge of the trail to fall in sickening plunges end over end from one ledge to the next on down the talus slope before finally stopping, a bloody, boneless hulk, a scant hundred feet from where I stood.

Standing there, shaken and unable to fully take in what was transpiring through the finder of my camera, I was witnessing the most starkly dramatic thing I had ever seen. In a short time four more elk came down, one at a time.

One cow came off the steepest portion of the cliffs and gained such speed in the descent that her body hit a big old dry fir snag about fifteen feet from the ground. It hit with such force, it literally exploded, showering the snow for yards with crimson blood; then it fell in a torn heap at the foot of the big stump with entrails streaming from the snags above.

Another young cow was pushed off the ledge by the one behind her, and she leapt bravely down to land belly deep in a snow-filled pocket. Her momentum carried her over the next cliff, but again she kept her feet under her, catching a ledge and then another with unbelievable agility. Her luck held, for she came down off that last rock face in a prodigious leap onto an inclining snow-drift. There her feet caught just enough on the frozen surface to break her fall before she slid on down to hit the talus, still standing. She recovered herself to come galloping down through a strip of scrub apparently un-hurt. I let out my breath in a long gasp unable to believe what I had just seen.

After a long pause during which she had witnessed the death of several of her bunch, the lead cow decided to try the icy gully ahead of her. Gathering herself, she galloped quickly across to come out on the easier going on the other side and safety. The rest of the elk began to follow, and as long as they took it at a run and kept going, it seemed easy enough. But then a cow stopped on the far side trapping a fine young bull on the chute with no place to go but down. Clawing for a toehold, he turned upward, trying to climb out on the shelves above, but it was too steep and slippery. For a moment he hung digging desperately with all four feet and then he peeled over backward down the gully. But he turned in the air to land with his feet under him glissading down the chute with showers of ice and snow crust streaming high on either side. Turning and twisting, never off balance for an instant, he shot down five hundred feet, turned off into the loose scree of the talus fan and came galloping on down past me without a hair out of place. What a magnificent picture he made—something I will be able to conjure up around evening fires for as long as I live.

The rest of the bunch made it to safe ground without further incident. When I shouldered my pack to head out across the flats toward home, there were two hundred feet of film in my pack recording the whole unbelievable occurrence. Most of it proved to be so totally bloody and objectionable nobody with any sense of feeling for an audience could show it, but there was enough to make an outstanding record, including the descent of the last bull.

I met Charlie and Dick on the way, still wide-eyed with the excitement of watching the spectacle through their binoculars. The bulls they had been trying to drive to me had gone in the opposite direction as I had guessed. When we reached home barely five hours had elapsed since we had left, but I felt drained and exhausted— about as tired as a man can get. One thing was obvious:

there are times when sheep and elk trails do not mix too well.

Rambling the mountains in winter can be exciting for other reasons, for the snow records the presence of many things: the delicate lacework of tracks left by a foraging shrew, the smallest mammal on earth; the sweeping pinion marks of a great horned owl spelling finis to a snowshoe rabbit; the paw prints of a pine martin questing for squirrels and grouse; nature's newspaper full of dramatic stories.

The coyote and the cougar added their track accounts to the mountain picture book that winter, for they were constantly present among the big game. We saw coyotes almost every time we went out, but as always the cougars kept well hidden during daylight hours.

The coyote is an opportunist, and while most of his diet consists of small game, the little grey yodeler misses no opportunities to take larger prey.

One morning I came over a hogback ridge among some scrub fir and pine to see about thirty mule deer and half as many bighorn ewes and lambs feeding on the slope in front of me. They were all mixed together, but when a coyote appeared out of some timber from a spot two hundred yards farther up the ridge, they were all instantly alert and the species began to separate. The sheep moved out onto a bluff directly opposite me, while the deer bunched up on some outcropping rock shelves about a hundred fifty yards above them. There were two bighorn lambs still with the deer. While I watched, all the animals stood with heads up, alert against a backdrop of frosted peaks and blue sky as the coyote came closer and closer. The coyote was a study of indifference just poking along as though breakfast could not be farther from his mind. But he was hungry, said the little red gods, and everything else including me was aware of it. The two lambs still with the deer were nervous and uncertain, wanting to get with their mothers, although their instinct warned they had best stay where they were.

The coyote reached a spot about fifty yards from the deer and perhaps a hundred twenty-five yards from the sheep, not directly between them but on the apex of a triangle pointing my way. Suddenly a big old doe started toward him with her hair all standing on end, her neck ruff actually slanting forward and her ears hanging down. She was the picture of menace and instantly the coyote stopped. This triggered the two lambs and they streaked down across a saddle toward the rest of the sheep. In a flash the coyote was at top speed cutting across to intercept them, and would easily have managed it had not two ewes, likely the lambs' mothers, come to meet them at a tearing gallop. It all happened in split seconds with beautiful timing and the coyote was suddenly aware that he was outnumbered. He stopped again, and while various animals sorted themselves out, he proceeded on down the mountain as though a belly full of lamb was the last thing he wanted. The deer and sheep stood for a while watching him go and soon all were feeding again.

Meanwhile my camera came to a sudden stop. When I opened it, it was to find the film had broken and was jammed in a tangled mess completely worthless. Such are the trials and tribulations of a winter photographer, sometimes long on opportunity but painfully short on results.

But such incidents are of fascinating interest just the same, an exciting example of the association of animals, the predator and its prey taking part in dramatic tableaux in unforgettable settings. Even with the film record lost, this was still worth a long climb to observe. Had either the sheep or deer panicked the story could have ended much differently, but these had been sagacious and brave enough to look after their own.

I have seen coyotes stalk and pursue deer many times, and always it is panic, bad conditions or some disability that insures their success. One time seven coyotes were observed pursuing a dozen mule deer, and after about a quarter of a mile of hard running with the coyotes twenty or thirty yards behind, a yearling fawn quit the bunch, veering off down a steep slope. It encountered deep snow in a strip of aspens and there the coyotes killed the unfortunate animal. Had it stayed with the bunch, it would likely have survived.

There are times when a sudden thaw and following freeze puts a crust on deep snow sufficient to hold the coyotes but letting the deer and sheep down. Then the advantage ratio tips away past normal to a point where the coyotes can kill at will.

In late May, 1927, we had a bad storm covering the mountains in and around the park with four feet of heavy wet snow. There was little wind with it, so there were very few places even on the most exposed ridge tops where the ground was whipped bare. When the skies cleared, the temperature dropped, freezing a heavy crust on the surface. The deer and sheep were trapped, unable to move.

The following evening a full moon rose to light a stark white world and the quiet air was full of the singing of coyotes collecting from near and far, traveling easily on the crust. All night long the yipping and howling continued as they killed and feasted. Next morning, Bert Riggall recorded thirteen fresh kills within sight of his glasses from the veranda of Hawk's Nest, the lodge here on the ranch. By the time the snow melted, the die-out among the sheep and deer was tremendous; for they are not constructed to deal with such conditions at this time of year, when their physical power is at its lowest ebb. Many were killed but many more just starved. The bad conditions of this storm were fairly local, so surrounding populations were sufficient to repopulate the region within a couple of years.

While wandering with our cameras among the bighorns, we often came upon the tracks, scratch marks and kills of cougars, although their numbers are always limited on any range. Unlike coyotes, they are not selective but kill at random, taking whatever animal offers the opportunity under any kind of condition. A big tom cougar will not hesitate to jump a full-grown elk or even a moose, although occasionally the ensuing fight goes against the cat.

At that time, my old friend Jim Osman, Fish and Wildlife officer stationed for many years at Fernie, British Columbia, in the famed East Kootenai game ranges before the coal strip miners desecrated it, accounts a rather unusual incident concerning a cougar and a bull moose.

The British Columbia Fish and Wildlife Department paid bounty on cougars then and encouraged staff members to hunt them with dogs. Jim was out one day trailing a big cougar with his fine pair of hounds up over a mountain ridge through deep snow. The cat's tracks led out onto a rim overlooking a timbered pocket and there the track story of a tremendous fight was written.

The cougar came out on a ledge almost directly over a big bull moose feeding among some alders and made a great leap down onto its shoulders. The bull rampaged down the slope into a thick stand of lodgepole pine where it succeeded in scraping the big cat off its back. Then before the cougar could escape, the moose reared and came down on it with its sharp, pile-driver hoofs. Only the deep loose snow of the sheltered pocket saved the cougar from being beaten into a bloody rag of bones and hide, for most of the time it was hidden and the bull's hoofs kept slipping off it. Finally the cougar made its escape.

It was too late in the day for Jim to trail the cougar any further, but he was back on snowshoes with his dogs early next morning. The hounds jumped the cougar within a quarter of a mile of the scene of the fight. Jim saw it climb a tree and said it moved like an arthritic old man just barely able to pull itself up from limb to limb. He shot it and upon skinning it, found the animal bruised from the end of its nose to the tip of its tail. No bones were broken but it had soaked up a tremendous beating.

All my life I have lived in country where cougars roam, and have often seen sign of them but rarely the animal that made them. These big cats are largely nocturnal preferring to lay up in daylight hours well hidden in thick cover or up amongst broken rock and do their hunting at night. Only twice in my entire experience have I had the chance to watch a cougar in the wild.

The first time was during the winter of 1958, when I was spending every possible day with the bighorns. Strangely enough the sighting was made almost within the village limits of Waterton. I was standing on the road glassing a bunch of sheep feeding on an open grassy slope just north of headquarters, when a movement caught my eye up on the cliffs above them. It was a cougar—a tawny golden brown animal with the typical mask over its face. It was stalking the sheep, coming down over the rocks toward them with all the fluid, silken grace these cats possess. Here and there it would freeze with only the tip of its long furry tail twitching, and then it would proceed. When it was still one hundred fifty yards from the sheep, an old ewe spotted it and almost instantly every sheep in the bunch had its eyes fastened on it. Again the big cat stopped, beautifully posed against the contrasting rock, and as is the way of most cats when a stalk goes sour, it saved its face by pretending sheep meat was the last thing wanted for lunch, and left. It had offered one of those magnificent sights potent with drama and sheathed violence, beautiful in its grace and stealth. The bighorns watched it go till it disappeared around a shoulder of the mountain, then they resumed their feeding.

The following summer I was climbing through a timberline larch park where the big trees were well spaced and the forest floor was carpeted with brilliant green snow grass. Just a few yards from the upper semicircular rim overlooking a deep basin, a flicker of movement behind a tree fifty feet ahead brought me to a sudden stop. Then from behind the tree out onto a sunlit strip of grass came a big tom cougar going straight away. Unable to resist I tried to get my camera out of my pack, but the faint sound was enough to alert the animal. The next instant he and I were eye to eye; then it ran in flowing bounds up around the rock rim, pausing here and there to look back before disappearing into the timber above.

The cougar is one of nature's most efficient and powerful killers. Unlike some of the bigger cats of Africa and the Orient, it kills with fine-honed skill rather than wearing its prey down by running or sheer weight. This big cat kills deer with the same nonchalance and dispatch a common house cat will employ on a rabbit. The deer are easy prey for them, but not the bighorn.

While hunting with the cameras that first winter I counted twenty-eight kills made by cougars and only three of these were bighorns. Many times I found fresh tracks in the snow where one of the big cats had tried for mutton, but the incredibly fast reflexes of the sheep usually saved them. If a cougar misses its first rush at a selected animal, it usually quits without any further attempt made on that individual or bunch. With deer as prey it rarely missed. It was always possible to tell when a cougar was in the vicinity of sheep, for when I returned in the morning to a place where I had left them the previous afternoon, they had often moved a mile or two. Subsequent investigation nearly always revealed fresh sign of a cougar.

One morning I struck fresh cat tracks in a light skiff of new snow where they led me to a story written sometime the previous night. The cougar came down directly over where six young rams had been bedded in the lee of some scrubby pines. Something must have warned the sheep at the last instant, for they had exploded in every direction about the time the big cat made his leap to catch one. It had been a near miss, for there was a tuft of hair lying on the snow where a claw had raked just short of its mark. The rams had split up into two groups and were long gone by the time I arrived on the scene. The cougar had made no attempt to follow, but had proceeded on down the mountain to kill a doe mule deer in her bed among some dwarfed aspens on a little bench. It had filled up on meat, buried the remainder and left by the time I reached the kill.

Cougars do not live exclusively on big game by any

means, for they miss no opportunity to take rabbits, grouse and porcupines. They seem particularly fond of porcupines and take them with varying skill. Sometimes they cripple themselves on the sharp, barbed quills to the point of being unable to hunt and suffering from starvation.

What amazed us most about the cougars was their amazing ability to stay out of sight, for in spite of the fact that we found plenty of tracks—sometimes very fresh—and the many hours we spent watching through powerful glasses, we rarely saw these big cats. Even in the protective confines of a national park they are very shy with only their tracks giving away their presence.

Sheep country in winter can be a very tough place for a man to work. We saw it at its best and its worst, but even at its worst there were always things of great interest to note.

13

In Pursuit of Ewes and Lambs

Over the months we covered a lot of mountains and encountered many bighorns. We could recognize by sight
about forty individuals and had been with them so often,
they showed no fear of us and often allowed us within
a range of feet. We were complimented thus by being
recognized as members of the society of wild sheep;
friends who never stepped across certain boundaries of
necessary protocol intentionally. It was a revealing and
exciting experience to find ourselves part of the world of
the bighorns and able to closely associate with these trim,
spectacular climbers in their mountains.

I found my whole outlook towards the sheep had
transformed into something vastly more interesting than
anything ever experienced as a professional guide and
hunter. No longer did the sight of a pair of magnificent
horns worn by an old ram excite any kind of covetous
desire to collect them as a trophy. Indeed, recording their
lives on film was so much more challenging and exciting

than hunting them with a rifle, there was no real comparison. This was the peak of endeavor, the absolute summit in the realization of exciting sport, plus the fact that it offered opportunity to introduce these animals in their true character to people in general by revealing some truth about the lives of these wild ones marking the joining links of life among the mountains.

No dead trophy could possibly compare with collecting such picture records as a bunch of big rams taking their ease high on some rocky ledge overlooking a vast sweep of wild valleys, where the soft murmur of rushing water far below was an undertone to the gentle singing of the breeze. To be allowed to sit and eat lunch amongst such a band of bighorns, while they gave us little more than a casual glance without stirring from their beds or pausing in the rhythmic chewing of cuds was sheer delight. Sometimes they reacted to our presence but generally their moves were more out of curiosity than any fear.

One day my friend Clarence Tillenius and I climbed up to take a seat in the midst of a bachelor's club numbering over thirty rams all taking a noonday siesta on a grassy bench among some scattered old pines. We sat in full view of them eating our sandwiches out of a paper bag passed back and forth between us. We noted one ram directly in front of us that was eyeing us with complete concentration. Never taking his eyes from us, he swallowed his cud and came slowly to his feet. His fixed curiosity was like a trance.

Clarence and I could not at first figure out why he was so interested in us. We were sitting side by side facing the ram, Clarence on the right and the open lunch bag on my left, its top stirring a bit now and then in the breeze. We never moved a muscle as the ram approached in an arc from the side till he was only three or four steps from the bag. When he stopped to look down at it, a little gust of wind rattled it causing him to blow through his nose and stampede. Instantly the whole bunch jumped to their feet and hit the ground running. We were suddenly alone.

"Now look what you've done!" Clarence drily observed. "You hurt his feelings. You might at least have offered him a cookie!"

While fraternizing with the lordly rams was fascinating, complete records of bighorn life required just as much work with the distaff side of the species, for the ewes offered much of keen interest, even if their profiles are a great deal less imposing to the eye.

One of the sequences I particularly wanted to include in the life story was ewes in spring and early summer accompanied by their new lambs. So when the warm winds began cutting the snow and ice off the mountains, I was constantly afield watching a lambing ground previously located up on the front of Black Bear Mountain. It was still too early, but I wanted to be on location when the ewes began to gather, so I spent my time observing and shooting the many changes synonymous with the blossoming of spring.

In the process I missed some epic occurrences. One morning I was driving up Pass Creek Valley after a wet, heavy snowfall. The road was just barely passable and the mountain slopes above were deep in new snow. Stopping the station wagon I was sitting on the tailgate with the camera screwed to the tripod in front of me, all set and ready to go. I had just shot a wide angle sequence of the peaks up valley glittering in the warm morning sun and was glassing for bear tracks, when a sharp swishing sound came to my ears. Right in front of me at the top of a big gully two thousand feet overhead an avalanche had cut loose. I jumped for the camera, slipped on some slush and kicked a tripod leg, and before I could get the camera leveled and realigned, the snow slide was coming to a stop right across the creek from me. The speed of a wet snow avalanche on such a steep face is incredible.

The gullies where springs flowed the year around were full of ice on the slopes and where these came down over cliffs, great aprons of blue ice were built up—thousands of tons of it—and there was one of these on a cliff face near the lambing ground. I spent two full days with my camera trained on it, for obviously it was ready to fall. Melting snow had undermined it with water, and a stream was gushing from under its lower edge. On the afternoon of the third day, I turned away for a moment to light my pipe, when a great roar suddenly filled the valley. I turned around just in time to see the last few chunks of ice subsiding in a heap at the bottom.

As experience has taught me, nobody but the fantastically lucky could hope to obtain such a shot; but my failure was an omen to more bad luck with ewe sheep on this location. Just about the time the ewes began to collect, the park trail crew began making a new trail along the foot of the talus slopes under the lambing ground. At the first dynamite blast, the ewes just evaporated, leaving me with no choice but to try to locate them.

For nearly a month I hunted steadily over a vast piece of rugged mountain country from the Continental Divide east to the edge of the prairie. It was frustrating and disappointing, for apart from rams and yearlings, I found no sheep. My long hunt had one advantage: I knew a lot of country where the ewes were not located, so one morning in the first week of June I rode my horse up onto a ridge in a portion of the mountains as yet unsearched. From a look-out point behind a rock I lay prone with glasses on a solid rest combing this wild trackless place.

Almost immediately I spotted ewes on some shelves directly across the canyon—females with tiny lambs at heel. Next day I was back, but made my approach up the bottom of the canyon on foot from its mouth to a timbered ridge flanking a steep draw dropping off the face of the mountain. Picking my way through a tangled mess of snow and wind-bent scrub where trees with trunks over a foot thick at their bases grew to a maximum height of no more than twelve or fifteen feet, I found a tortuous route that finally took me to a spot where I could see. It was very hot and still, and the deep shade of my look-out under a gnarled pine was a welcome comfort. At first the sheep appeared to be gone, but then I spotted them directly opposite me almost completely camouflaged among broken ledges, as they all lay in various attitudes of repose in shady spots as they too sought shelter from the hot sun.

About noon the lambs began to get restless, moving about to nibble at various bits of herbage, skipping about among the ledges like mountain sprites and occasionally nudging their mothers. One lamb jumped on its mother's back as she lay snoozing, spilled off to one side as she got up and then began to suckle. One by one the ewes got up to let the lambs nurse, and then they began picking their way down to a strip of new green growth beside the bawling little stream in the bottom of the gully directly in front of me about one hundred fifty yards away, where they began to feed. As they came closer I began recognizing certain individuals among the twenty-two matrons being watched. One we knew as Broken Horn, for her right horn was twisted and short probably from an injury from a falling rock when she was a lamb. Another was a fine handsome old grandmother all of twelve years old that I remembered particularly for a fine picture she had given me at a salt lick in Pass Creek Valley about three months before. She was making a bid to renew her youth for she had a sleek healthy new lamb at her heels. These were the ones that would have ordinarily lambed on the Black Bear Mountain location, but now were miles north clear over a range of mountains. Finding them was like relocating old friends and filled me with anticipation of getting the lamb sequences I wanted. But when I slowly stood up to reveal myself, every ewe froze in her tracks staring fixedly at me. When I moved a step or two towards them, they bolted up the mountain wild as hawks.

Why they were so spooky is something I cannot account for, except the possibility that the blasting back on their favorite mountain had been such a traumatic experience, they had developed a distrust of men. I could only guess, but for five straight days they led me on a merry chase all over that rugged slope without a single chance to expose a foot of film. Just as soon as I appeared every morning they assumed watchful poses, all strung up to run if I came too close. It was frustrating and disappointing, but it sparked a determination to regain their confidence. I would have liked to camp in their vicinity, but the weather was uncooperative and besides, the ticks were out in legions—all ferociously hungry. Then several days of rain kept me off the mountain, and when I found the sheep again, they were moving up across a pass heading back towards Pass Creek.

Next day I drove up towards Red Rock Canyon and climbed to intercept them, but it was noon before I found them bedded on the comb of a spur ridge high above timberline. Again they spooked when I came close and were lost in a jumble of ravines at the head of a tributary creek.

It is big country. Day after day I climbed and hunted, sometimes finding the bunch and just as often unable to locate them. They were drifting towards a ford across Pass Creek leading up toward Ruby Lake on the east face of Blakiston Peak, the highest in the park. But more wet weather and melting snow had put the creek into flood, making the ford dangerous to the lambs, so they veered west along the flanks of ridges for several miles.

On Dominion Day, July 1st, I was high on the slopes overlooking Red Rock Canyon sweating under a pack in the hot sun on a traverse across a wide grassy slope. Earlier that morning I had got a distant glimpse of my elusive nursery from across a canyon, and now I was hoping to find them among the folds of this slope. Tired and frustrated, I sat down to rest and use the glasses.

The road up the valley below was alive with cars; the campground and picnic area in front of the ranger's station at Red Rock was like an ant heap crawling with tourists. This beehive of activity was full in the field of my glasses, when suddenly out of the timber in the midst of the crowded picnic ground came my friends the ewes all lined out like a string of packhorses. Mincing along like a bunch of proud mothers showing off their spring clothes and their new offspring, they marched straight

through the crowd with scarcely a glance one way or the
other, down Red Rock Creek, across it just above its fork
with Blakiston Brook, and then tripped blithely across the
wooden footbridge. There they disappeared in the timber
heading up onto Mount Anderson.

I just sat there for a while feeling like a rejected
parent, unable to believe they would do a thing like this
to me. It was enough to make one wonder if photographers are not sometimes fated to be treated like pariahs
infected with some kind of plague, or the butt of a long-
winded joke. It was certain sure this bunch was hellbent
to make a fool of me, or so it appeared. It was bad enough
to see them walking through a crowd of noisy people,
but the crowning touch to the whole unbelievable charade
was their use of the bridge. As I headed for my vehicle
and home, I was low in my mind. But I vowed to myself
that I would catch up to that pixilated bunch and film
them till my supply ran out, if it took the rest of the
summer and I wore their legs off to the knees!

School was just out, so two days later six of us were in
the saddle with a string of packhorses trailing; a family
pack trip heading up towards Twin Lakes near the Divide
miles ahead of my errant bunch of ewes and lambs. It
was a renewal of acquaintance with old trails for Kay, but
a brand-new experience for our five-year-old daughter
Anne. Up on Chief, a venerable and reliable old trail
horse, she looked like a bee on a big stump sitting her
saddle with her short legs sticking almost straight out
and her eyes sparkling with excitement.

It was a beautiful sunny day when we started, but by
the time we were two hours up the trail storm clouds
were blowing in from the west. We were in heavy timber
when the storm broke over us with thunder and lightning.

Anne was close behind me and before the first big drops of rain began spattering the dust of the trail our slickers were on. A few moments later the rain turned to a deluge of quarter-inch hail. I backed my lead horse in under a spruce and wise old Chief tucked himself in close beside me, while the rest of the string found similar shelter from the force of the stinging hail. While hailstones trickled down through the limbs of our tree, Anne sat wide-eyed as thunder rolled and rattled among the peaks around over the steady drumming of the hail. It was a wild initiation for a little girl on her first day in the mountains, but she showed no fear.

It was over in a few minutes and the sun came out again as we rode up the last mile to our campsite. When we reached it, I stepped off my horse and turned to lift Anne down. She was sitting her saddle with tears streaming down her face, quietly sobbing. When I asked her what was the trouble, she whispered that her feet were cold. Upon investigating I found that her little riding boots had been sticking out from under the skirt of her slicker and were full of hailstones to the top. Pulling her boots off, I rubbed her feet and then held her close with them tucked inside my shirt against my skin, and in a little while she was again her usual cheerful self, dancing around full of questions as we pitched the tents and Kay began putting together a hot supper.

Shortly after sunrise next morning Dick, Charlie and I climbed up a low pass on the trail going south towards Lone Lake, while I turned east from the summit along the crest of a ridge towards Mt. Anderson. At noon I was on top of a sharp spur overlooking a deep wild basin on the north slope, where a bull moose was feeding in a beaver dam far below. To the south and east along the sunny flank of the peak a vast scree slope stretched away for over a mile. I was eating lunch between sessions of glassing, when a movement in a patch of shintangle away out on this slope caught my eye. It was a band of ewes and lambs.

Finishing my sandwiches I headed out towards them in a traverse putting me above their level and succeeded in getting close enough to identify my elusive friends. Not wishing to upset them, I retreated to give them a chance to locate and settle down. I planned to return the following morning, but low clouds hid the mountains till noon, and when I got back up on the ridge, they had moved. Baffled by this will-o'-the-wisp bunch that had given me the slip so often, I hunted for them all afternoon without any luck, then headed for camp as the sun dipped towards the west.

From the top of a promontory overlooking the pass, I sat down once more to glass the country. The air was still, the sky spotless and the late sun was throwing great mountain shadows across the canyons and slopes to the east. Here and there the peaks wore silver collars of mist draped on their shoulders as though standing in deep contemplation waiting for something to break the great quiet. It was one of those timeless and breathtaking moments when the silence seems to stretch to eternity.

Then something appeared on the very crest of the peak on the Divide above the lakes. I put the binoculars on it to find a single ewe, silhouetted in black against the blue sky, tiny in the distance. More and more appeared out of a gully to join her. It was my missing bunch. Sometime during the day they had passed along the ridge and I had missed their tracks and now they were standing on the crest of the backbone of the continent. Which way they would choose to go from there

—south or north—was strictly a guess, but I surmised it would be south. It would not be west, as that is not sheep country. In any event they would likely bed down after the long climb and not move again till morning.

At sunrise I was on a trail leading up onto the Divide to the north of camp—Sage Pass, where I would either intercept the bunch or find their trail if they chose to go north. But not a sign of them showed anywhere until I topped the peak where they had been spotted the evening before. Fresh beds were evident on the shale there and their tracks pointed south down slope to the upper rim of a cliff. From there I could look out across a vast stretch of mountains away south into Montana, impressive peaks shining with snow and ice. On the far eastern horizon, the rim of the prairies showed in purple and gold. Somewhere closer along the ridge of the Divide were the elusive ewes and lambs. Directly under me down toward the South Kootenai Trail, Dick and Charlie were moving up through a larch park toward a bunch of rams. At least they were getting some footage while their father wandered like Ahab in his obsessional search for the fabulous white whale across these frozen waves of mountains; a hunt which so far had yielded nothing but tired muscles and aching feet.

All day I rambled and hunted down along the spine of the Divide, finding rams and a few goats and enjoying a distant view of a fine silvertip grizzly, while white clouds sailed by overhead on the wings of a gentle breeze. It was late afternoon when I turned back toward the distant camp. Again the ewes had vanished like a puff of smoke. The stars were beginning to show when I reached the tents, bone-tired and disgusted; but still there under my chagrin was the recognition of a challenge and a determination fitting snug like a well-worn buckskin jacket.

This sheep pasture was huge—folded, gullied and rifted by canyons and peaks, a vast rugged land full of a thousand hiding places and many choices of route. Knowing I must have missed them somewhere in some sheltered hollow or hidden bench, I was back in the same country the following day with no better results.

Several days later I climbed a peak on top of the Divide far to the south and came on some fairly fresh sheep beds. The tracks in the pawed-out beds were those of ewes and lambs. There had been no rain since they had been made and the dust on the edges of the hoof prints had caved in a bit, softening their outline and making them about twenty-four hours old. But no further sign of the sheep could be located in spite of much scouting and looking, although a faint trail revealed that they were still headed south. About mid-afternoon I climbed back up on the crest of the peak to use my glasses and after about an hour, the lenses picked up a familiar, tiny silhouette outlined against the sky on another peak far to the south at the extreme limit of my visual range. It was the old ewe leading the bunch, for I counted them as they all climbed over the skyline to disappear down the eastern side.

They were now far out of reach of our Twin Lakes camp, so we packed up to return to the ranch, where we luxuriated in hot baths, read the mail and restocked the grub boxes. Then we headed back into the mountains, this time going up Cameron Creek to its confluence with Rowe Creek and thence up to a big basin at its head. It was late evening when we got camp set up on the edge of a big timberline meadow. We rolled up in our sleeping robes that night to sleep soundly after a long day on the trail.

The sun was painting the mountains in rose and gold next morning by the time breakfast was over, and I stepped out in front of the tents to have a look with the glasses. Almost immediately I spotted sheep near the top of the ridge to the north toward Paradise Basin within five hundred yards of where I had seen them last —twenty-two ewes and fourteen lambs. Again we were ahead of them, and I couldn't help wondering just how far this chase would lead us.

There was one way to find out, so the boys and I caught our horses, loaded the cameras and headed up the long steep trail toward them. From the time we left camp, we stayed in sight all the way, pausing often to rest our horses and let our elusive models look us over. It was pleasantly warm and by 10 A.M. we were about five hundred yards beyond the sheep and a bit below their level. Tying the horses in a clump of scrub, we set the cameras up, checked the loadings and then eased out along an inclining sheep trail toward them. They completely ignored us, and when we had come within a hundred yards we climbed up onto a slight swell on the slope, which was all covered with coarse red talus. At this point a nurse ewe lying with a dozen lambs directly in front of us got up, stretched and then turned her tail to us as she began to feed. The lambs with her lazily quit their beds to move aimlessly about until finally the whole bunch was up. There was querulous blatting culminating in all the lambs going to their respective mothers to suckle with enthusiastic bunting of udders and shaking of tiny tails. All the while the whole bunch gave us small attention in complete reversal of their previous attitude toward me.

After feeding, they all moved off across the slope up

onto the face of a cliff. We followed and when they stopped we were practically mingling with them. My old friend, Broken Horn, even came a few steps toward me to stand within a few feet gazing up into my face with her wise golden eyes. Her look was bland and friendly, not a hint of malice or mischief in it, no guile, but completely innocent and trusting, and I couldn't help wondering why she had made herself so hard to approach for so long.

Then up on the face of the steep rock the lambs suddenly burst into frolic. Standing on the edge of nothing with my hip pockets hanging out over eagle thoroughfare, I filmed a sequence of lambs pouring themselves off minuscule ledges, one behind the other to land on similar ledges below, bounce to another and another and then reverse their way back up onto the rock face. Sometimes when the rock was a bit less than perpendicular, they set their feet and slid using the friction of hoofs and the hair on the back of the legs to lower themselves. They looked as though they were being let down smoothly and surely by invisible strings, a marvelous display of control and agility. The school of the wilds had taught these ones well and the cameras recorded a real nugget of bighorn life as they performed all around us. Our only problem in collecting this beautiful picture on film was our precarious perches, for a slip would have been disastrous.

All morning we loaded and shot film till we had none left in our packs that was unexposed. Then we sat and ate lunch while watching the sheep string out heading back to their original bedground where they all lay down.

This was the culmination of a long hunt—seventy-four days of continuous searching with few breaks, forty-three of which had been in steady pursuit across close to fifty miles of tough and rugged mountain country under all kinds of conditions from blazing sun to hailstorms. We were honed down to hard muscle and bone, but right there as we sat watching the ewes and lambs, the hard work and frustration was forgotten. For a while I had been banished from the herd, but now it felt wonderful to be back and know the collected film had something we had never filmed before.

During the days that followed we found all kinds of bighorns all over the mountains around camp. Almost any time of the day they could be seen from the tents. Almost never when we climbed did we fail to approach sheep. It was a golden bonanza of opportunity and we made the best of it.

After two weeks of this idyllic activity in spotless weather, we tore ourselves away, for horse feed was getting short on the meadows around camp. So we packed up to move farther south up over the ridge back of Cameron Lake and on down to the timberline meadows overlooking Boundary Creek.

Here it was possible to see sheep, deer and goats as well as smaller game; pikas, ptarmigan and marmots, all on the same slopes. By this time Anne was a veteran packtrain traveler and enjoyed many new adventures with us. During our fortnight there where our tents were pitched on a big flower-strewn meadow on a timberline rim overlooking a great sweep of mountains, glaciers and brilliant blue-green lakes across the valley, she moved, ate and slept in a fairyland full of wonders.

We had a distinguished visitor at this camp, Ken Weaver, a member of the editorial staff of *National Geographic*, who had flown out from Washington, D.C., to join us for a few days. He is a highly experienced world traveler, but at that time had never had the opportunity to participate in a wilderness packtrain camping trip. One afternoon we went over a pass between camp and Carthew Lakes. On a steep rocky slope between the lakes he was with Anne and me when we found a covey of rock ptarmigan—a mother with a brood of half-grown chicks. As usual these birds were unafraid and were keeping just a few steps away. Anne was fascinated with the young birds and wanted to pick one up.

"Daddy, I want to catch one!" she exclaimed.

"If you stand very still till I tell you to move, and wish very hard, you can do it," I told her. "But we will all have to be very still and you will have to wish very hard."

She accepted my suggestion without question. Ken cocked a quizzical eye in my direction, no doubt wondering what I had in mind. But he went along with the game and stood watching while the mother and her young ones clucked and chirped around us. I was watching the ptarmigan but also keeping an eye open for a pair of eagles that were nesting high on the face of Carthew Mountain, hoping one would choose to fly into view. After a few long minutes, just as I was beginning to wonder if my little play was going sour, an eagle showed up sailing majestically on a thermal out over our heads perhaps two thousand feet up. Almost instantly the mother ptarmigan gave a low chirring noise in her throat, which meant danger and freeze where you stand to the chicks. They all froze absolutely still in their tracks.

"Now!" I said to Anne. "You can pick one up."

She stepped towards one of the young birds and before the astonished eyes of our guest, she did just that, to her vast delight. He covered his surprise a bit by becoming very busy with his camera but laughed with appreciation when I pointed to the eagle and explained. It was another one of those times when the opportunity comes for a bit of showmanship, very simple but impressive.

Years before, Bert Riggall had confounded me by stepping down off his horse to pick up a full-grown ptarmigan when an eagle had flown low over our heads on top of a high open pass. They know they dare not try to fly for cover when a hunting eagle is in the vicinity, so they just freeze thus allowing their grey summer feathers to camouflage them among the rocks.

Bert had passed over the end of the divide that is the end of the trail of all men on earth, but his little granddaughter was sharing some of the fun and adventure made possible by knowledge he had left behind in these mountains he knew so well, with a new-found friend from the concrete canyons of a big city. Thus does life and the joy of living continue by being passed like a baton in a great relay race.

14

When Horns and Opinions Tangle

The collection of footage was almost complete, at least sufficient to tell a comprehensive story of bighorn life. There were still two key sequences to obtain; one being a knock-down drag-out fight between two old herdmasters, and the other a fairly close-up series illustrating the activity of the lambing grounds in spring including, if opportunity allowed, the actual birth of a lamb. Then with a few short sequences to tie some of the sequences together the film would be about as complete as one could hope for without spending unlimited time and expense. For when dealing with such a complex subject with all its threads of ecological significance, each one dependent on the other to a greater or lesser degree and every one being of shining interest when properly interpreted, it would be quite possible to work on a specie's life history for twenty years. Of course, from any kind of practical viewpoint, such an expenditure of time and money is utterly impossible, so we were bound to keep the record dwelling on high points rather than losing ourselves in details, however fascinating they might be.

So with these things in mind and the bighorn mating moon due to rise in late November and reach its full apex in December, I once more prepared to be with them during this cold inhospitable portion of the year.

Some lessons had been learned the previous winter. One of these precluded the purchase of a new and much heavier tripod complete with bubble levels and ball and socket head attachment allowing the camera to be instantly leveled on rough ground with a minimum of wasted time and sometimes costly vibration showing on the film. Nothing is more aggravating to a viewer than trying to look at a picture that dances on the screen. The previous tripod had been well constructed but too light for the winds of sheep country; at a certain wind velocity it vibrated like a tuning fork with a movement imperceptible to the eye through the viewfinder, but when the work print was projected, the much-enlarged picture revealed the tremor. The work print was being continually appraised by the studio as it came in, and all such technical shortcomings were supposed to be reported immediately, but the foundation had not provided their technician with an adequate viewer. So he missed spotting this slight wind vibration until several thousand feet had been wasted. This kind of thing is frustrating to the point of anguish, for it reflects directly on the photographer and about all he can do is make belated adjustments and suffer. Fortunately most of the sequences involved could be replaced, but this was small comfort.

The Bell and Howell cameras were rugged and dependable, and I had learned to live with their shortcomings, although there were many times when the spring-wound drives left something to be desired when the action was fast and prolonged. When warm these cameras would expose twenty to twenty-two feet, but cold the best they would do was fifteen to eighteen feet even when winterized—not nearly enough when prolonged sequences were desired. Electric drive cameras would have been more satisfactory, but also considerably more costly and cumbersome.

By wrapping the film in an old wool sweater at room temperature before leaving home, the film breakage problem had been partially cured, although even when thus insulated in my pack, it rapidly got cold when loaded in the camera when the wind chill was low and penetrating.

One thing troubling my mind and giving me little comfort was the failure of the foundation to renew my contract. Originally I had requested and been orally granted two years to do the film work in the field, but when my contract form came it was for only one year. I had taken it back unsigned and had a meeting with the founder and head of the foundation to discuss this oversight. He explained it was foundation policy not to give out contracts of over one year and promised mine would be renewed. But now, even though the directors expressed satisfaction with the film to date, my renewal was months overdue and my requests were met with smiles and more promises that were never kept. The prospect of not having time to finish the job worried me considerably, for this was a dream project I had wanted to do for years. Never before had I tackled any kind of assignment without being able to finish it, and the prospect chilled me more than the wintry blasts howling down off the peaks.

This somewhat personal matter of business that involves such efforts is not recounted in any attempt to justify my shortcomings, but only to point out that it takes more than equipment and skill to be successful in such endeavors, it also calls for a tough and determined settlement of initial terms. As with most creative people, my mind naturally drifts toward the problems of the field and the clear, comprehensive production rather than the mundane, though highly necessary, business arrangements. My tendency was more toward trusting people than foreseeing possible failure through the absence of ironbound clauses in contracts; nor did I let the possibility of personality conflict cloud the issue unduly.

This was my mistake, for this photographer thus exposed himself to a much wider range of perils beyond the possibility of slipping on an icy ledge and going over a cliff while pursuing my fleet-footed wild models across the rugged slopes of the Rockies. And most likely my associates must have also found it somewhat frustrating dealing with a man who refused to be shackled, one who really knew and enjoyed a truly free life, while their work harnessed them to desk chairs. The results could have been illuminating, but unfortunately took on the shape of something rather ugly. It was a strange thing to observe otherwise intelligent men turning their backs on the value of the end product in an attempt to exercise the same 9 A.M. to 5 P.M. control they held over office employees. Sometimes I was reminded of Kipling's lines of verse: "When east is east and west is west, and never the twain shall meet."

With a lot of my problems still hanging unsolved, I headed back up onto the wintry slopes to enjoy the honest and straightforward association of the bighorn rams just as they were beginning to drift down from among the storm-hung peaks toward lower ground and their trysting with the ewes. Now, because of the material previously collected, I could afford to be selective; so many long hours were spent just drifting with the sheep, watching and always ready but actually doing much less shooting with the cameras.

There were about sixty head of bighorns in the ten-mile length of Pass Creek valley that winter; most of them individuals easily recognized through long contact, so it was never very difficult to approach them. It was interesting to note the difference weather and temperatures exerted on their movements. Just before a storm there is always much movement and tendency to play among animals. After the storm arrived with its lower temperatures and wind their lives fluctuated between feeding and bedding down in shelter. When temperatures are low they expend as little energy as possible in any kind of unnecessary movement. If I chose to disturb them when they were bedded down in cold weather, they displayed their displeasure at my intrusion by turning their tails to me, so that about all that could be seen through the view finder was a collection of very expressive rumps effectively conveying the idea that I was about as welcome as a skunk at a garden party. The same thing happened if I stayed too long in good weather. Their first indication of their boredom with my company was showing me their white rumps, and if I persisted they always took some excuse, however slight, to rush off and leave me standing all alone in the midst of scenery empty of sheep.

But sometimes they displayed some considerable interest in having me appear, seeming to welcome the break in the general humdrum of their daily activities on their mountains. One morning I climbed up along a big game trail around the end of a ridge looking for a bunch left there the previous afternoon. When I spotted them they were feeding on some grassy shelves among cliffs six or seven hundred yards up the slope. I was standing there wondering if the rewards would anywhere equal the hard work of climbing to them, when they spotted me and all lined up on a rim looking down. Then a fine, classic-featured old ewe leading the bunch suddenly broke into a run with all the rest strung out in line at her heels. At top speed they came racing down the slope weaving back and forth as they took advantage of the ridge's contours. Never out of sight and without a break in stride, they came barreling right up to me to halt line abreast like cavalry horses on parade inspection. Just before they started I had been watching them through the view finder, admiring the picture they made against the blue sky, so I had a complete sequence of their descent. Now they stood as though waiting for instructions at a range of thirty feet.

It was by no means the first time I had been thus greeted. Clarence Tillenius, having once observed this interesting sidelight to my prolonged association with the bighorns, remarked, "I think you must have them on your payroll!"

When rutting season came around in November, activity among the sheep was, as always, very much increased, and as it moved towards its December peak, they tended to ignore me almost completely. As always the weather was unpredictable, cold and blustery with very limited time in sufficient light for photography. Consequently by the beginning of the week before Christmas I still had not collected the fight between big rams. I had obtained some short shots, several at extreme range involved with fights, but these were inadequate and too brief.

Bedevilled by the rotten weather and poor luck, I

was feeling low in my mind. But I kept on hunting steadily in spite of conditions that were often next to impossible, hoping for a break.

Then one morning the sun rose in a cloudless sky. It was still and mild without the slightest hint of a breeze. As sometimes happens, I was savoring a premonition of success as I headed up into sheep country—a feeling that my luck was finally breaking for the best.

Stopping at a vantage point to play the glasses over the slopes, I immediately spotted a big ram traveling alone across the front of a mountain high above Pass Creek. Even at a range of at least a mile he had an aggressive, trouble-hunting look about him—a certain arrogance of bearing that is the hallmark of a questing male. He dropped from sight near the head of a twisted side canyon, so I climbed into its mouth and then up along its flank to intercept him. At the top of a jutting buttress I sat down to use the glasses but the ram had vanished nor could I find any other sheep. Then I picked him up again still traveling towards a saddle on a ridge to the west. Retracing my steps to the main valley bottom, I circled to head him off.

Around the end of a hogback ridge, I found what I hoped to see: another fine big ram escorting a ewe half a mile above me on a narrow bench in line with the route the first ram was taking. The ewe was obviously just coming into oestrus.

My climbing was inspired that morning. My boots literally flew over the ice-draped ledges, and within minutes I was on a rim just below where the ewe and ram were located. Pausing to let my breathing steady down, I screwed my camera down on a specially constructed shoulder stock allowing fast handling, then eased up over a broken rimrock just in time to see the opening flourishes of an epic battle.

Many men have willingly paid thousands to get within rifle range of just one such ram. Here I crouched within fifty feet of two mighty old warriors with massive horns so engrossed with each other they paid me not the slightest attention. They stood facing each other with heads held high and proud, the sun glinting from their golden eyes. Both were magnificent specimens, not a hair of their rich dark grey coats out of place. There was no preliminary circling or displaying of horns as usually goes with such confrontations; it was like a prearranged duel where both contestants were all primed and ready for battle. The photographer's prayer came to mind, "Let there be light!," and the sun shone brightly from directly over my right shoulder.

Then both made a few quick steps toward each other, reared with front legs hanging straight and necks bowed and when only a few steps apart, hurled themselves forward to meet in mid-air with a jarring crash, horn to horn—a crash that rang in the still, clear air. The impact was so terrific that their bodies whiplashed and the arrested inertia of their weight jerked their heavy neck hair and short tails straight up. Then they stood dazed momentarily by the shock, staring away off at nothing, before swinging on their heels to maneuver into position for another charge. Again and again they slammed into each other with shattering bangs sounding like two hardwood logs swung end to end together. Once I saw horn splinters fly through the view finder and a new yellow scar appeared on the frontal boss of one of the defender's horns. Occasionally one would stop to jam the massive frontal curls of his horns into the ground with a twisting motion, while he pawed the dirt like an angry bull. Several times they came within a few feet of me and once I was looking up at them as they met almost over my head. They paid me no more attention than if I had been a stump. I shot, rewound and shot again and again, then reloaded with flying fingers to shoot some more. My hands were steady even though excitement boiled and bubbled all through me.

Again and again the shock of their collisions seemed to knock them half-senseless and they stood with glazed eyes looking at nothing. Finally both rams began to tire, and the fighting took a more sinister turn. Shouldering into each other, they circled and pushed striking with a forefoot up under each other's flanks. Several times a flying hoof narrowly missed an opponent's big, hanging testicles. This strategy was not nearly so precise and accurate as the meeting of horns and no damage resulted, although doubtless if one of the striking hoofs had connected the battle would have ended right there.

After several such exchanges, the defending ram suddenly broke off the engagement to head away down the mountain. The challenger followed closely for a way, making no attempt to close again, but apparently just being sure his rival was leaving for good. Then he turned back up the slope to claim the prize.

According to all the rules of romance, it would be fitting to say this triumphant warrior came to his light of love and they disappeared together into a high, rocky trysting place to court and couple happily among the fastness of the peaks. But he got back just in time to see the cause of all the uproar disappearing over the skyline closely pursued by an ardent young four-year-old ram. This young fellow had been attracted to the scene by the sound of horns banging together, and while the big rams and I were engrossed with the fighting had slipped in to steal the ewe away. What the precocious one lacked in weight of weapons, he made up in nimble feet and the principles of a hijacker. The victorious old gladiator just threw a look after them and proceeded to absent-mindedly nip off a couple of mouthfuls of grass, too tired to pursue. I passed him my unspoken sympathy and headed down the mountain almost as exhausted as he, for the climbing and the excitement had burned up a lot of energy. But I was jubilant, for a scene had been recorded on the film that no other could surpass.

It was the climax of a long hunt that had stretched over seventeen months of living with the bighorns every day the weather allowed, winter and summer. Although I did not realize it at the moment, it was also the end of my bighorn life history recorded on a total of fourteen thousand feet of film. Naturally, not all of it was usable, but six thousand feet was good; not a bad average for such shooting.

My work had been successful as far as it was allowed to go, but somehow through no real fault of mine, the whole program collapsed. Although he knew nothing of bighorns, the man who had invited me to take on the assignment, and thus displayed a remarkable insight and imagination towards possible values, had lost interest. Like many newly arrived princes of finance, he reveled in power and control of those people associated with him. My resistance to anything that infringed on the freedom so necessary in creative work infuriated him to a point of complete breakdown of communication between us. I worked harder and went farther than I have done in my life before or since to restore it, for in spite of his lack of understanding of my way of life there was much to be liked about this man. I felt if we could just establish some mutual understanding we could work together, for I knew he had an opportunity like few men of my acquaintance to provide the means of recording natural history in a way it had never been done. But office politics and jealousy had reared their ugly heads, compounding my difficulties. There were limits of self-respect and principle beyond which I would not take a step.

He made appointments to meet with me—appointments that meant more than three hundred miles of driving to keep—then left me sitting in his waiting room for hours, without apology or explanation. After two such frustrating and fruitless experiences I knew it was no use trying any longer.

For one reason or another, the film has never been produced. Had I merely been a custom photographer with no real interest in outcomes, it would not have been such a bitter pill to swallow, but I am a naturalist and conservationist with a very real interest in what my work can accomplish. It was a sad finish to what was a grand experience and a wonderful opportunity.

But no clouds that darken a man's life are so impenetrable that nothing good can come even from their shadows. Nothing can blot out the experience and what is not to be seen of the pictures can be brought to life in these pages; the pitting of one's wits and muscles against the intelligence of a great animal living among the crags of the Rockies. Life is exactly what we wish to make of it and the stumbling blocks often temper a man's capabilities.

So today when I stand on my doorstep looking out over a vast expanse of bighorn country, every fold of the mountains means something as islands of cloud shadows drift across the rugged slopes; for my feet have taken me across almost every yard of it and a good deal more besides. Nothing can take that away, and it has been a warm and wonderful pleasure to recount the years of looking and adventure.

About the Author

Andy Russell was born in 1915 in Lethbridge, Alberta, Canada, and describes his education as "limited formal education, considerable Rocky Mountain variety." Both contributed to the success of his book *Grizzly Country*, acclaimed by critics and naturalists alike as a major contribution to the study of the great bear, and later to the similar popularity of his books *Trails of a Wilderness Wanderer* and *Adventures with Wild Animals*. He has spent his entire adult life as a trapper, broncbuster, hunter, rancher, and professional guide and outfitter, and more recently has become a full-time author, environmental consultant and photographer. He has also produced lecture and television films, acted in television documentaries and contributed to a radio series. He is widely known as a popular speaker and lecturer on natural history and conservation. In 1976 he received the Julian T. Crandall Award for conservation effort, the highest of its kind in Canada, and in 1977 he was honored with the Order of Canada from the Governor General with the approval of the Queen. Mr. Russell is married to the former Anna Kathleen Riggall, and they have four sons and a daughter.